The Protectors' Handbook

Gerrilyn Smith

LIBRARY
LRC

BAAF
ADOPTION
& FOSTERING

Published by
British Association for Adoption & Fostering
(BAAF)
Saffron House
6–10 Kirby Street
London EC1N 8TS
www.baaf.org.uk

Charity registration 275689 (England & Wales) and SC039337 (Scotland)

British Library Cataloguing in Publication Data
A catalogue record for this book is available from the British Library

ISBN 978 1 905664 47 4

Project management by Shaila Shah, Director of Publications, BAAF
Photograph on cover posed by models by istockphoto.com
Designed by Andrew Haig & Associates
Typeset by Fravashi Aga
Printed in Great Britain by The Athenaeum Press
Trade distribution by Turnaround Publisher Services, Unit 3,
Olympia Trading Estate, Coburg Road, London N22 6TZ

BAAF is the leading UK-wide membership organisation for all those concerned
with adoption, fostering and child care issues.

Contents

Preface to the second edition   1

1   **Introduction**   3

    General characteristics of sexual abuse   9

    How to protect children   11

2   **Recognising signs and indicators**   16

    Under-5 age group   21

    5 to 12 age group   32

    12 to 16 age group   42

    Following up your concerns   49

3   **Reducing the risks and helping children to tell**   54

    How to talk about sexual abuse   55

    Following up your concerns   65

    What to do if a child discloses sexual abuse to you   69

4   **Establishing a context for recovery**   78

    What the child needs   80

    What you need   84

    Blocks to being an effective protector   91

    Maintaining the context for recovery   96

5   **The emotional consequences of sexual abuse**   99

    Areas of concern   105

    Dealing with the consequences   125

6   **The healing process**   129

    Beginning the healing process   130

    Getting professional help   133

    Different types of work to help children heal   147

    Managing challenging behaviours   151

    Conclusion   154

7   **Sexual abuse and trauma**   156

    Afterword   172

    Appendix: Useful organisations; books; videos 186

Acknowledgements

I would like to acknowledge the wonderful creative clinical team I work with at Alder Hey – Pete Harmsworthy, Family Therapist; Frank McGuire, Bev Harding and Simon Lewis, Psychologists; Hazel Gearing, Mark Carlin and Margaret O'Hanlon, Social Workers and my Treatment Foster Care colleagues. Together, we have taken both old and new ideas, melding them into a service that I think is truly inspiring and innovative. We privilege relationship in our work and try to support primary caregivers in working with children and young people. We also maintain a political perspective in understanding the wider social factors that impact on children's mental health like poverty and social injustice.

I would also like to acknowledge my son's contribution to my own thinking. When I first wrote this book he was only a child and now he is a young man. All of the children, young people and parents who have helped bring the material alive remain in my thoughts and heart.

Thank you

Gerrilyn Smith
September 2008

Note about the author

Gerrilyn Smith is a Consultant Clinical Psychologist and Systemic Psychotherapist. She has worked in a number of settings, including voluntary agencies, the health service, local authority and private sector provision – all focusing on child protection services. She ran the Department of Health Postgraduate Training programme in Child Sexual Abuse which aimed to develop assessment and treatment services for children and families where sexual ause was an issue. She has lectured and published widely in the field, and has advised on a number of public enquiries into safeguarding issues.

Preface to the second edition

I am delighted that BAAF has decided to reprint *The Protectors'
Handbook*. If I reflect over my career, I can see a huge change in
the whole area of child protection in general, today referred to as
"safeguarding", and sexual abuse in particular.

Clinically, sexual abuse still presents within services. For example,
at a time when the Liverpool Child Protection Register recorded
eight per cent of registered children (29) under the category of
sexual abuse, our figures in a Child and Adolescent Mental Health
Service for Looked After Children showed 26 per cent of referred
children (77) with a recorded (but not necessarily substantiated with
a finding or criminal conviction) history of sexual abuse (May 2008).

When looking at resources, many date from the period when sexual
abuse was still very much on the agenda. I have not found much
new published material, but the increase in resources via the
internet is incredible. It may be that adults and children are more
likely to use this medium to find help.

When considering the changes I have made in my clinical practice,
I can see the influence of research on trauma, and specifically its
impact on the developing brain. I also see sexual abuse within a

matrix of other adverse childhood experiences such as domestic violence, physical abuse, neglect, emotional abuse, parental mental health, criminality and drug and alcohol abuse. It is easy for the sexual abuse story to get lost – especially in the presence of other overwhelming experiences that have not been subjected to such scrutiny and legal debate.

I still remain firmly rooted in clinical practice, reminding myself and my colleagues of our primary duty to our clients within a mental health context. I remain sceptical about legal solutions to family difficulties or a child's exposure to significant harm.

In keeping with my own longevity in the field, I am also more mindful of life cycle issues, by which I mean issues of abuse over the life cycle and across generations. I am also aware of the impact of secondary post-traumatic stress in doing this work, and perhaps how fears for our own psychological well-being contribute to the minimisation of discussions regarding sexual abuse.

There have been huge changes in our exposure to information via the internet. I have to confess to little professional expertise in this area, but for vulnerable children and young people this "window to the world" can make sexual exploitation seem almost inevitable. Sex continues to be a commodity.

This handbook focuses specifically on sexual abuse. In doing so, it does not diminish or deny the significant harm caused by other forms of abuse. With a focus on sexual abuse there is a subtext that sexual intimacy based on love and true connection is potentially the best healer of all. If we do not address this intimate violence, then future intimacy is less likely to succeed in providing the secure and loving context to create a different future.

Gerrilyn Smith
Liverpool, 2008

Introduction

In the 1990s, there was an increasing awareness of sexual abuse of children and its long-term consequences. This resulted in a number of services focusing specifically on child protection for children currently growing up, as well as providing resources for adults who had been sexually abused as children and who were still struggling with the after-effects.

Despite this growing awareness that sexual abuse does happen, there is still much controversy about the scale of the problem. The figures given in the first edition of this book suggested that 47 per cent of the population would experience some form of unwanted sexually intrusive contact before 18 years of age, with one per cent experiencing sexual abuse by a father or father figure (Kelly *et al*, 1991). In a study looking at the experiences of 16–74-year-olds (Office for National Statistics, 2000), two per cent of males and five per cent of females reported an experience of sexual abuse. The huge variations in figures relate to definitions of sexual abuse and how the figures are gathered. The NSPCC website, at www.nspcc.org.uk, provides useful information on understanding the research on incidence and prevalence. Official figures, however, represent only a small proportion of sexual abuse. In a more recent (2000) survey using a computer-assisted interview with a random sample of 2,869 young people aged 18 to 24, 21 per cent of females and 11 per cent of males reported some form of childhood sexual abuse, with a smaller proportion reporting childhood sexual abuse involving contact (16% and 7% respectively) (Cawson *et al*, 2000). Childline's figures (2005/2006) show that eight per cent of calls made to them were about sexual abuse and 86 per cent of the children calling about sexual abuse indicated that they knew the person abusing them (Childline, 2005/06). For the past ten years, bullying has been the most common reason that children ring Childline. But sexual abuse is also a form of bullying. The same process of trickery and intimidation is present. The violation of a relationship is also a key feature.

There has also been much publicity regarding what is termed False Memory Syndrome, where people recover memories of sexual abuse that they previously repressed and which are considered to be untrue by others. It is unfortunate that the issue of false memories should receive so much public attention, since this detracts from the struggle that survivors, supporting protectors and professional child protection workers have mounted to get sexual abuse recognised in the first place. There are instances where false allegations are made, often by children who were not believed in the first place. There are probably instances where a false memory is induced by bad practice, but this is rare in my experience.

The existence of sexual abuse in childhood cannot be denied. Child protection workers and those professionals involved in working with sex offenders know from their experience that the problem is widespread. They also know that considerable resources will be needed for the foreseeable future both to protect children from future sexual abuse and to help adults and children, perpetrators and victims, to recover from the devastating consequences. It is accepted that most perpetrators sexually assault a number of children. In figures released by the Home Office (2006), there were 29,973 individuals on the Sex Offenders Register. It is not possible to distinguish those who have targeted children.

Since the first edition of this book was published in 1995, there has been a massive increase in the number of people cautioned or charged for offences relating to child pornography. Of convicted child sex offenders, 60–70 per cent only target girls, 20–33 per cent only target boys and 10 per cent target both. The majority (80%) target children known to them (Grubin, 1998).

In recent research on adult mental health (Mental Health Foundation, 1993), as many as 50 per cent of women and 20 per cent of men receiving psychiatric treatment were found to have a history of childhood sexual abuse. The situation remains much the same now as it did when I wrote the first edition of this book. While most adults are not abusers, to be non-abusing when sexual abuse is so widespread, and its consequences so disturbing, is not enough. We must all play an active role in *reducing the risk of child sexual abuse occuring*. This book can be used to support foster carers who have children placed with them where sexual abuse may be an issue.

A network of adults surrounds all children in the community. Within this network are both possible protectors and perpetrators, with the former outnumbering the latter. Yet possible protectors are frequently unable to either prevent sexual abuse or promote recovery from the experience for any one child because rather than acting as protectors they function as non-abusing adults. This book aims to transform non-abusing adults into protectors by providing information about sexual abuse that will help to reduce the risk of sexual abuse occurring and aid the recovery of those who have experienced it.

This book is a practical guide to effectively protecting children and helping them to recover from an experience of sexual abuse. It is a book for adults who want resources and information so they can feel more confident in identifying and raising the issue of sexual abuse in their families and their communities. It is also, but by no means exclusively, intended to be useful to professional child protection workers.

The first section of the book concentrates on ways to reduce the risk of child sexual abuse. It includes advice on talking to children *before* sexual abuse happens. This is based on the belief that it will be easier for children to tell adults about inappropriate or uncomfortable contact if there has been previous discussion about it. If you are used to talking to your child or to children close to you about difficult issues, you will have a base on which to build the trust and empathy that are necessary for the child's recovery process, should sexual abuse occur. This is especially important for those involved in fostering. Discussions with your own children prior to any placement ensures that your children will know how to deal with inappropriate sexual questions or advances from foster children. This part of the book gives clear advice on the signs and indicators that might suggest child sexual abuse and discusses in detail how to decide whether sexual abuse is the most likely explanation for what you have observed or been told. Many children come into the care system without the issue of sexual abuse having been considered, for example, because the neglect they experienced was so great or because one or both of their parents had severe alcohol or drug problems. Once in placement, many foster carers observe behaviours which cause concern and which are highly suggestive of inappropriate sexual experiences. There follows clear guidance about what you can do if a child you know tells you about being sexually abused, or if you feel the signs and indicators do suggest sexual abuse.

> **We discovered that when young people and children disclose sexual abuse, that is not the end as we had been led to believe. It is, in fact, only the beginning – the first step on the long road to recovery.**
> *Sue and Dave*

The second section of the book concentrates on the recovery process. The emotional consequences for a child of being sexually abused are described, including some of the more challenging behaviours that the child may display. Suggestions are made on how to deal with challenging behaviours. It is extremely important to establish a good context for recovery for a child who is trying to deal with an experience of sexual abuse. There is clear advice about what constitutes a good context for recovery and how you can help establish it.

This book draws on my experience as a child psychologist working in the field of child protection. I have worked in many different contexts – including a telephone counselling line, a local child mental health clinic, a social services department, teaching hospitals and a private sector girls' residential unit. I now head up a Child and Adolescent Mental Health Service for looked after children in Liverpool based at Alder Hey Hospital. The book is also based on the experiences of survivors of sexual abuse, both adults and children. Names and some identifying details have been changed to protect confidentiality but the examples given are from my clinical work.

For various reasons, agencies that deal with child sexual abuse cannot be wholly effective in reducing the risk of sexual abuse or helping the child and possible protectors when sexual abuse becomes apparent. Most resources focus on the apprehension of offenders, with an inordinate amount of professional time going into investigations that never get anywhere near the criminal courts. For example, in one area within one London borough over the period 1990–92, there were a total of 1,476 referrals for joint police and social work investigation. Of those, 590 (40%) were referrals for sexual abuse. Criminal charges were brought in 91 cases, 15 per cent of the total number of referrals for sexual abuse. Of that proportion, only six convictions were secured, three of which did not involve a prison sentence.[1]

There is a significant difference between the number of reported or referred cases and those considered substantiated. For example, a comparison of three countries showed that the ratio of referrals to substantiated cases was considerably lower in England, where only five per cent of reported cases were considered substantiated,

---

1   See also Kelly et al, 2005.

compared to 20 per cent in Australia and 18 per cent in the United States. This was for all forms of child maltreatment. Despite the difference in substantiation rates, all three countries showed a similar breakdown in terms of sexual abuse. Roughly 10 per cent of all referred cases of child maltreatment were sexual abuse (extrapolated from the NSPCC figures). Despite the fact that overall totals for referrals of children and young people in need of a child protection plan (previously this would have led to registration on the Child Protection Register) rose over the period 2003–07, rates for sexual abuse as a category have been dropping.[2]

A study into children's perceptions of professional responses to sexual abuse identified 202 children, who were all considered to have been sexually abused, according to the professionals working with them. Of those cases, only one in three resulted in criminal prosecutions, and only one in four perpetrators were convicted (Prior *et al*, 1994). This represents an enormous amount of time and effort going into the investigative process, producing a very small return in terms of the number of convictions secured.

The impact of this can be seen in what I have termed the professional retreat from sexual abuse, including the identification and naming of it. For example, a recent referral regarding a child described a range of behaviours including the ten-year-old taking his penis out and rubbing it under his school desk when the classroom assistant was nearby. When the professional attempted to confirm this information by saying, 'So the child is masturbating in inappropriate places,' the referrer retreated and said, 'Well, I wouldn't exactly call it that'.

Before even reaching the stage of a formal investigation, someone has to recognise that sexual abuse may be taking place. Behaviour is often the first indication of something happening that requires

---

2   See www.dcsf.gov.uk for data collected in England. Similar data are collected for
    Scotland, Wales and Northern Ireland and can be found at www.dataunitwales.gov.uk
    (for Wales), www.scotland.gov.uk/Publications/2007/09/20161825/11 (for Scotland) and
    www.dhsspsni.gov.uk/community_stats_06.pdf (for Northern Ireland).

investigation. If the child has told someone, they need to be
believed and the adults around the child will need to protect them
from further sexual abuse. The criminal justice system alone does
not fulfil these functions. It is therefore essential that the adults
surrounding children in their day-to-day lives are able to talk about
sexual abuse issues, recognise the indicators that suggest it may be
happening, and feel powerful and informed enough to act on the
child's behalf.

General characteristics of sexual abuse

Defining sexual abuse can be difficult, even if you have experienced
it yourself. The desire to deny it has happened or to minimise its
effects is often overwhelming for all concerned. Even with a lot of
help and guidance, it can still be difficult to identify and articulate.
However, there are some general characteristics of sexual abuse that
are well documented and repeated in study after study.

The vast majority of sexual assaults on children are committed
by people known to the child (Cawson et al, 2000). Assaults by
strangers are the minority of cases, but because they do not carry
the same reporting restrictions, we hear more about them in the
media. The single largest category of offenders within families is
brothers and stepbrothers (38%) followed by fathers (23%), uncles
(14%) and stepfathers (13%) (Cawson et al, 2000).[3]

There is increasing evidence of unwanted sexual contact being
perpetrated by other juveniles, especially brothers (Cawson et al,
2000).[4] Several studies show that a significant proportion of sexual
abuse (25–35%) is perpetrated by young people on other young

---

3   The study cautions that the numbers for children abused within the family were small,
    so the figures need to be viewed with caution. However, the general trend of brother as
    perpetrator is reported elsewhere. They also recorded a small percentage of sexual
    abuse perpetrated by mother figures: i.e. 4%.

4   ChildLine figures (2005/6) suggest that 9% of children calling about sexual abuse had
    been sexually abused by another child. Of children calling about their own abusive
    behaviour, 47% were boys abusing siblings. Available at: www.nspcc.org.uk.

people (Lovell, 2002). Young people sexually abusing other young people was overwhelmingly the most common pattern of sexual abuse outside of the family.[5] There is now considerably more research on sexual abuse by women of both boys and girls (Saradjian, 1996).

Sexual abuse can start at any age. It rarely involves one episode of sexual abuse but more often involves many episodes, and many acts. The age it starts at can be difficult to identify as it often begins with appropriate touching that gradually becomes inappropriate. Sex offenders purposely disguise sexual touching to be confusing both to the child who experiences it and, perhaps more importantly, to anyone who inadvertently observes it. With very young children, it often occurs around bath time, during toileting or nappy changes, and at bedtimes, where a benign cover of appropriate touching can confuse any possible protectors. Many children will date the start of their abuse from the point at which penetration is attempted. However, it would be safe to assume that by this time there has been other, more ambiguous, touching that has occurred as part of the softening-up or grooming process.

Force, whilst always implicit in child sexual abuse, is rarely used. The role of violence is more evident when the perpetrator is not known to the victim. In the majority of cases where perpetrators know their victims, powerful threats and sometimes bribes ensure co-operation. The close proximity and ongoing relationship between perpetrator and abused child mean that the threats can be reinforced periodically, the child can be reminded by the perpetrator of the consequences that disclosure will bring, and bribes can be used that may be especially tantalising to a particular child.

Sexual abuse is a premeditated crime. The individual who commits it has thought about it and planned how to do it. (Even attacks by strangers, in which the target is randomly chosen, are planned and premeditated.) For me, this has remained one of the most disturbing features of this work.

---

5   The study by Cawson *et al* put the percentage at 70%.

He'd, like, bring me out and be all nice, but I always
knew it was going to happen at the end. He'd, like,
be all nice and buy me everything that I wanted, you
know, and in the end just do it all over again.

He used to come up to the school to pick me up – like,
my mum would be up there, my sister, but he wouldn't
bring them two home, he'd just give me a lift home,
you know – he would always take me out, he wouldn't
take the rest of them out. All the things he bought me
and did for me, it was like I owed him something.
Alison

Many people feel more comfortable believing that sexual abuse is
a momentary, impulsive lapse of self-control. But the reality is quite
different. It is especially important to remember this when working
with juveniles who engage in sexually harmful behaviours. Many
adults play down such behaviours, without considering in detail
what has happened or looking for evidence that can help them
make an assessment about how serious the young person's problem
has become.

How to protect children

Much work has been done to identify factors that contribute to an
episode of sexual abuse. David Finkelhor (1984) has identified four
factors that are critical in any episode of sexual abuse. They are:
(1) the presence of an individual with a motivation to sexually abuse
children; (2) that individual overcomes their own internal inhibitors
against such behaviour; (3) the protectors surrounding the child; and
(4) the child's own resistance.

Effective intervention needs to be directed at each of these
identified factors, both before any sexual abuse happens and to help
those who have already experienced sexual abuse. Such intervention
should include treatment resources for sex offenders, for the

children who have been sexually abused and for the adults – often primary caregivers – who are trying to help the child recover and who frequently need help themselves in coming to terms with what has happened.

Teaching children to be assertive, to say no and to get away (addressing Finkelhor's fourth factor above) does not adequately deal with the subtlety and complexity of sexual abuse by known, often trusted, adult caregivers. The bulk of the protective task should rest with adults, with children taking only a developmentally appropriate level of responsibility for protecting themselves.

There is much debate about whether convicting sex offenders is the best form of protection in the long term. This could partially address Finkelhor's first factor, by removing potential perpetrators, but there are many convincing arguments to suggest that in and of itself the conviction of sex offenders is not enough to protect children in the future.

As we have seen, most sexual abusers are not convicted. Of those who are convicted, many are given a non-custodial sentence, and others serve relatively short sentences. Very few receive any psychological help to stop them from reoffending. Whilst they may return to families who know about the sexual abuse, many will move to new families where knowledge of their past sex offending behaviour is not available or fully understood.

> He's gonna do it again – if he gets away with it, he's gonna do it again. People like him don't stop. And now that he's got away with it once, he's gonna think he can get away with it again . . . He's got children – he's probably doing it to them.
> *Alison*

Research also suggests that custodial sentences, far from preventing further sex offending behaviour, can increase it (Morrison *et al*, 1994). There is evidence to suggest that some sex offenders are organising to share ideas, strategies to avoid detection, and helpful hints on how to offend, as well as swapping or sharing their victims. It is likely that time in prison gives a sex offender an opportunity to network with others who have a similar interest in sexual abuse. Not all convicted sex offenders participate in the Sex Offender Treatment Programmes run by the prison and probation services.

Therefore, increasing the effectiveness of all the possible external inhibitors to sexual abuse must be an integral part of protecting children. Children need to be surrounded by a community of adults amongst whom the majority are possible protectors (Smith, 1994). Sex abusers are often very skilled at rearranging the child's network so that they are closer to the child than any possible protectors. It is therefore crucial that possible protecting adults have all the skills and information necessary to recognise the signs of sexual abuse and know what to do if it occurs.

Many people, including some professionals, still believe that children lie about sexual abuse or make up allegations; that only strangers sexually molest children; that it only happens once; that mothers always know if it is happening; that it is easy to prevent or stop; that only certain types of people sexually abuse children; that it only happens in certain communities or certain families; that it isn't so bad really; or that if children didn't like it they would tell. But like it or not, sexual abuse is commonplace and will touch all of us, either personally through our families and communities or professionally in our work, especially if we work with children.

Non-abusing as a stance is no longer good enough. As adults, we must move from a passive, non-abusing stance to a more proactive, protecting stance, in order to protect our children.

References

Cawson P, Wattam C, Brooker S and Kelly G (2000) *Child Maltreatment in the United Kingdom: A study of the prevalence of child abuse and neglect*, London: NSPCC

ChildLine (2005/06) data available at: www.nspcc.org.uk

Finkelhor D (1984) 'Four preconditions: a model', in Finkelhor D, *Child Sexual Abuse: New theory and research*, London: Collier MacMillan

Grubin D (1998) *Sex Offending Against Children: Understanding the risk*, Police Research Series Paper 99, London: Home Office

Home Office (2006) 'Keeping communities safe: multi-agency public protection arrangements', press release issued 23 October 2006, quoted on www.nspcc.org.uk, Key child protection statistics

Kelly L, Lovett J and Regan L (2005) *A Gap or a Chasm? Attrition in reported rape cases*, Home Office Research Study 293, London: Home Office

Kelly L, Regan L and Burton S (1991) *An Exploratory Study of the Prevalence of Sexual Abuse in a Sample of 16–21-Year-Olds*, London: Child Abuse Studies Unit, PNL

Lovell E (2002) *Children and Young People who Display Sexually Harmful Behaviour*, NSPCC Research Briefing. Available at: www.nspcc.org.uk/Inform/research/Briefings/sexuallyharmful behaviour_wda48213.html

Mental Health Foundation (1993) *Mental Illness: The fundamental facts*, London: Mental Health Foundation

Morrison T, Erooga M and Beckett R (eds) (1994) *Sexual Offending Against Children: Assessment and treatment of male abusers*, London: Routledge

Office for National Statistics (2000) 'Lifetime experience of stressful life events: by type of event and gender, 2000', *Social Trends 32*, London: Office for National Statistics

Prior V, Lynch M and Glaser D (1994) *Messages from Children: Children's evaluations of the professional response to child sexual abuse*, London: NCH Action for Children in partnership with the Newcomen Centre and the Bloomfield Clinic at Guy's Hospital, London

Saradjian J (1996) *Women who Sexually Abuse Children: From research to clinical practice*, Chichester: Wiley

Smith G (1994) 'Parent, partner and protector', in Morrison T, Erooga M and Beckett R (eds) (1994) *Sexual Offending Against Children: Assessment and treatment of male abusers*, London: Routledge

2

Recognising signs and indicators

This chapter examines some of the signs which suggest that child sexual abuse may be happening. Clearly, this is important information for primary caregivers, including parents, grandparents and other relatives. It is also important for teachers, nursery nurses, foster carers, residential workers, health visitors, general practitioners – virtually anyone who comes into contact with children and young people.

Adults should know about these indicators, because expecting children to verbally articulate what is happening to them when they are being sexually abused places too much responsibility on the child. Sometimes it is known or suspected that a child has been sexually abused but no one has talked about it with them. The child's behaviours – reactions to their experience of sexual abuse – can continue and people forget how those behaviours arose in the first place.

> He used to say to me that if I ever told, my mum would hate me and she'd, you know, do this and do that. And it was also embarrassment, and you blame yourself – you're thinking, 'I should have said no, I should have

> **done this' to have stopped him. So I thought that I'd
> get the blame if I told . . .**
> *Alison*

There are many valid and compelling reasons not to tell. The fear of
being disbelieved is one of the most common. It is also important to
recognise the seriousness of the threats made to children if they do
tell. Alison had to live with the fear that if she disclosed, her mum
would hate her. If abuse is occurring in the context of a domestically
violent relationship, then the potential consequences do not need to
be spelled out to the child. Many children are prepared to sacrifice
themselves for what they believe to be in the interests of family
peace.

> **I couldn't tell Mum – I felt I was letting her down . . .
> 'cause after what he had told me, I didn't know what to
> expect from her. I thought she wouldn't believe me . . .
> it sounded too unbelievable . . . she might turn round
> and say, 'Why would he be doing it to you?'**
> *Alison*

Adults in contact with children must have the courage to guess,
or at least to be curious, when children show signs that they are
confused or worried about something. For foster carers and
residential workers, this may be easier because they are unlikely
to have an emotional connection or tie to the alleged perpetrator.
However, they often feel disempowered and restricted from having
conversations with children or young people about sexual abuse
because of perceived legal constraints. This is really unhelpful. I have
come to believe that talking about your lived experience is far more
important than a criminal prosecution or civil proceedings. I have far
too much experience of criminal proceedings never taking place, or
failing, and of civil proceedings dragging on for years, causing
further trauma to the child by leaving them in an intolerable
position of uncertainty.

> It's easier if someone else says it, rather than coming out with it, like, you know, someone's touching you.
> *Alison*

> Karen [social worker] sort of guessed something was going on, and like, she helped me bring it out in the open. I think, like, she, like, was picking up hints and everything, and, like, she was trying to piece them together and then she just came up with this and asked me and through the tears and everything I said yes.
> *Natasha*

But it is also important to know that not all children are worried by sexual abuse. This may be because they are very young and do not understand that it is wrong; or because in their family, it is the norm; or because they have no experience of it not happening. Natasha was abused not only by her biological father but also by her stepfather, so it was not until she lived with her foster family that she began to understand that fathers do not have sex with their daughters.

> I think it really took a lot for, like, me to, like, think 'This is wrong, this is not supposed to happen . . . ', 'cause they were family and you look up to them and think of them as an example. It really takes a lot to, like, understand that they do it, and they're not supposed to, and they know they're not supposed to.
> *Natasha*

There are some behavioural signs that are very suggestive of sexual abuse. In the table at the end of this chapter, there is a list of such signs and indicators arranged by age. This list should be used as only a guide. It is most likely that if sexual abuse *is* happening, there will be a number of signs and indicators from all of the categories that have been present for quite some time. The categories are arranged into red alert to indicate high risk, green for moderate risk and blue to indicate low risk.

In reviewing the signs and indicators originally published, I could feel a cautiousness come over me and a desire to remove the list completely. However, I have decided on balance to leave this list as originally published. I think we need to maintain our curiosity when children show distressing and disturbing behaviour – and sexual abuse is only one hypothesis among others to be considered. I still think of a child's symptoms as a coded message, probably because of my work as a family therapist. I see them as telling me something that can't be put into words.

Ryan is a 14-year-old boy in a foster placement. He was referred by his foster carer because he was soiling – hiding poo and dirty underpants daily. He was also making allegations that adults were looking at him in a strange way; sometimes he said they had sexually abused him. The foster carer wanted to help him with his behaviours. I asked if Ryan had ever been sexually abused because his symptoms made me think he might have been. He had moderate learning difficulties. I wondered if his soiling was an indication that he was not in charge of his bum or his poo and whether his constant fears of being looked at, sometimes followed by clearly false allegations, were connected to an allegation that had not yet been made. I saw his behaviours as a way to start a conversation about sexual abuse, whereas before it had been seen as lying. He was seen as "a boy who tells lies" and, perhaps more problematically, "makes false allegations". His soiling was seen as part of his learning difficulties and general laziness. But with a change of focus, the foster carer was able to ask more questions and have hunches about what Ryan might be trying to tell her. This resulted in Ryan making disclosures about being sexually abused when he was much younger and before he came into care.

The following discussion regarding the indicators is divided into different age ranges, focusing primarily on the red alert signs for each group. When assessing indicators of sexual abuse, it is important to take into account the child's stage of development. What may be appropriate behaviour for an older child may indicate a problem for a younger child, or vice versa. Also, the material will need to be adapted for children with learning difficulties, who may have a chronological age much higher than their cognitive age.

Remember that, regardless of the number of indicators, it is still important to fully investigate your concerns by gathering more information and being prepared to have them either confirmed or disconfirmed. I would now refer to this as curiosity, and encourage you to be open minded but maintain your curiosity until whatever is happening makes sense to you and the distressing or disturbing behaviour is occurring less frequently or has ceased. Sometimes a police investigation is begun, but no charges are brought. Often people see this as meaning no sexual abuse has happened and they stop thinking about the issue. For the child or young person and those that care for them, this can be very unhelpful as the psychological distress expressed by symptomatic behaviours remain. The symptomatic behaviours can result in a referral to a Child and Adolescent Mental Health Service. Sometimes the cause of the symptomatic behaviours are forgotten. The distressing behaviours are seen as evidence of a psychiatric illness. This is a shift from environmental causation (risk of significant harm/safeguarding issue) to mental illness (medical model of illness) without recognising the importance of the experience that sexual abuse played in developing the distressing behaviours in the first place. For example, much self-harm, running away from home or addictions can have their roots in sexually abusive experiences that are undisclosed or disbelieved.

Leyla is a 12-year-old girl who had been in treatment for three years. It was known that she had been sexually abused in her family of origin, although this was not discussed in her therapy in any detail. The reason given was that Leyla did not talk about it or spontaneously raise it. The sexual abuse happened when Leyla was very young. Throughout her therapy, Leyla carried on hurting herself and she often needed to be admitted to hospital. Her foster carers felt it was important that Leyla's experience of sexual abuse was talked about but they didn't feel confident about doing so. Leyla's new worker, in conjunction with her foster carer, began their work together by talking about Leyla's sexual abuse – making a connection between Leyla's current symptoms and her past experience.[1] This therapy was much more direct and open about the sexual abuse as something known about and available for discussion. By the second session, Leyla began talking about her experiences of sexual abuse, prompted by the more direct approach of her worker. By session ten, there were no further episodes of self-harm.

Waiting for children to bring up their sexual abuse puts a huge responsibility on them. They need caring adults to lead the way gently and tentatively towards making sense of past experiences. This is especially important if the child has also been traumatised. In a way, you need to lend them your mind to put things together. This aspect of sexual abuse is dealt with in Chapter 7, where I discuss the impact of trauma on children who have been sexually abused.

Under-5 age group

There are some characteristics of children in this age range that will help possible protectors to be more alert to the indicators of sexual abuse. This is especially important because a significant proportion of these children will have little or no language.

One of the indicators will be physical signs, although many types of sexual abuse do not leave any physical indicator. If you notice any injuries to a child's genitals these should be investigated immediately. Many mothers of babies who have been sexually abused notice differences in the child's genitals or anus, and sometimes this will be pointed out to health visitors, GPs or nursery staff. These kinds of concerns should always be taken seriously and investigated further by a paediatrician with knowledge of sexual abuse and who is prepared, if necessary, to be involved in court proceedings. No parent wants their child to be medically examined more than is necessary. It is therefore important that the right

---

1   The foster carer was offered the training published by BAAF (Hellett and Simmonds, 2003). If the CAMH LAC Service I work in does not have a group running, we then run the training as individual seminars for foster carers.

professional does the examination. Otherwise, the wrong opinion regarding risk can be given, important medical evidence may be lost, and the appropriate medical follow-up may not be made (such as testing for venereal diseases).

Despite limited verbal ability, children in this age range often do tell adults about being sexually abused. Because their disclosures are so brief, often containing only the essential elements of who did what, many adults do not take them seriously or give them credence. In this age range, children tend to be naïve disclosers. They are too young to know the consequences of disclosing and often do not really understand the true meaning of secrets. If they were asked to tell you what they were told not to tell you, it is likely they would oblige.

Spontaneous disclosures in this age range frequently occur in a context where one would least expect them. They contain essential detail but little elaboration, and the child often does not realise the significance of what they have said. For example, one nursery worker asked her group of ten two–three-year-olds what they did before they came to nursery in the morning. One little girl, Evelyn, said very clearly, 'Daddy fuck my bum'. The nursery worker, who was quite shocked by the child's utterance, said 'Pardon?' and the child repeated what she had said.

In a significant number of cases in this age range, the child will show a range of behavioural disturbances that will be noticed by primary caregivers. One of the largest single categories of these disturbances is sexualised behaviour. Masturbatory behaviour is one example. Many children in this age range masturbate without this being an indication of sexual abuse. It becomes a red alert sign when it has a compulsive quality to it: the child does it in preference to other activities; normal tactics of dissuasion are unsuccessful in getting the child interested in something else; and it occurs in a range of different contexts, not just, for instance, prior to going to sleep. It can also involve putting objects into either the vagina, the penis or the anus.

By the time the child has reached the age of five, most primary caregivers will have helped their child to learn the social etiquette of masturbatory behaviour. The child may have received strong inhibitory messages about doing it at all. Most will have been encouraged to do it privately in safe places like their bedroom. Masturbation is a perfectly normal behaviour and should not cause alarm in parents. It can be compared to other behaviours which are antisocial in public, such as nose-picking, which most parents manage to steer children towards doing less conspicuously and in approved places.

When masturbatory behaviour has qualities which make it a concern, it is important that primary caregivers make an effort to discover why it has become a preoccupation with the child. Clearly, in a child with no language, this is problematic. However, it can be a signal that someone, and most usually an adult, has made the child's genitals a focus of attention. Children can experience sexual arousal if their genitals are stimulated and an adult who knows this can exploit the physical dependence of the small child. Compulsive masturbatory behaviour would not arise from accidental contact with a caregiver.

Often compulsive masturbatory behaviour is accompanied by anxiety, other signs of distress, or hyperarousal. It is important that if this is the case adults who care for the child notice the behaviour and report it. In Evelyn's case, the nursery staff had observed her masturbating in the nursery. She was not private about it and the behaviour was accompanied by loud grunts and groans from the child that sounded quite strange and unchildlike. This child also had a fear of having her nappy changed and would scream to keep it on.

Compulsive masturbatory behaviour is a red alert sign of abuse. Other behaviours that fall within the red alert section of the list include sexualised drawings, developmentally inappropriate sexual knowledge, and overt sexual approaches to other children and adults.

Primary caregivers of children in this age range will have seen many drawings. If children draw people and mark in their genitals, it is important to be curious as to why this part of the body is receiving such attention at this time. For example, a young boy started drawing all of his people with breasts following the birth of a sibling. His mother was breastfeeding and breasts become significant enough to mark on his drawings. After a while he stopped. Clearly, this is not a case of sexual abuse and indeed the little boy had no other signs or indicators of sexual abuse.

Heston and Norleen – two children involved in a case about contact where their mother was worried that their father had sexually abused them – began their interview with investigators by drawing pictures of themselves. They both drew large circles for people with arms and legs coming from the circle. Eyes, nose and mouth were carefully marked in, and then in between the legs they both noted 'ting-a-lings'. This spontaneous introduction of genitals in their drawings needed to be followed up.

Primary caregivers often have a good intuitive understanding of what constitutes developmentally appropriate sexual knowledge. You will probably know what your child knows about the "facts of life"because it is most likely that you will have told them yourself. Children begin by asking questions about where babies come from. The mechanics of how the baby "got in" and how the baby "got out" will come later. Children in this age range are preoccupied with excretion and how their private parts work in relation to weeing and pooing, since toilet training occurs in this age range. Some children will have discovered pleasurable feelings from touching their genitals. However, specific knowledge regarding sexual acts, in particular, knowledge of penetration and/or oral sex, is extremely unusual in this age range.

Primary caregivers should be able to identify where sexual knowledge has come from. It is unlikely to come from accidentally viewing a pornographic film (one common explanation) or accidentally walking into their parents' bedroom and seeing them involved in sexual activity. A one-off accidental view like this is unlikely to produce the kind of inappropriate sexual behaviour described in this section. Inappropriate sexual knowledge manifests itself as a preoccupation by the child, something they talk about and make reference to constantly – often something they are trying to understand. If a parent has elected to give an under-five-year-old sex education, it is unlikely that it would lead to behavioural disturbances. If the sex lessons came with demonstrations, this would constitute sexual abuse. It is for children themselves to discover how their bodies work, not for adults to show them.

Direct, often explicit, sexual overtures are a red alert indicator. Children in this age range do not know that sexual contact between adult and child is wrong, and if a child has been initiated into sexual behaviour, they may try to engage others in such activities. For example, these extracts from a foster carer's diary demonstrate clearly not only overt sexual overtures but also the four-year-old child's sexual preoccupations.

> *7 January*
> **Martin tried to lick my genitals through my clothes whilst sitting on the floor between my legs. Martin says that he does this to Mummy and Daddy . . .**

> *14 January*
> **Martin showed me his penis. When I said why did I want to see that, he replied because he loves me. He went on to say when you love someone you can show them your penis. His mum says so.**

Overtures to other children need to be interpreted differently from the normal curiosity among children regarding differences between boys and girls. However, if children are involved in overtly bullying another child to participate, attempting penetration or putting objects inside each other's genitals or anus, this needs to be followed up.

Indicators which are not in the red alert section include situation-specific fears, such as bath times, toileting and bedtimes. These are often the situations that are exploited by individuals who have a sexual interest in children. Children can also show person-specific fears. For example, Jasmine was afraid to be bathed only by her father. When anyone else bathed her, she was fine; when her father bathed her, she was frightened. Over time, this fear can become generalised. Norleen's fear of going to the toilet became so severe that she became frightened to go at all. She would tell her mother that often when she was going to the toilet daddy had hurt her bottom. In both cases the situation-specific fears suggest that some inappropriate touching had occurred in these contexts. They are green indicators because there are benign explanations – it could have been, for example, that Jasmine's distress was a result of her disliking the way her daddy washed her hair, or that Norleen's distress was to do with the way her daddy wiped her bottom.

Developmental regression, where a child returns to a previous stage of development (e.g. bed-wetting when they have been previously dry), is another sign of stress. It is considered a blue sign because children in this age range frequently show developmental regression in response to a wide range of stressors including, for instance, the birth of a sibling. Equally low on the index is aggressive, withdrawn or clingy behaviour. These are all indicators of stress, but in and of themselves are not indicative of sexual abuse.

Jasmine showed a whole range of symptomatic behaviours from across all three categories of risk. Before making a verbal disclosure, she demonstrated compulsive masturbatory behaviour, night terrors, fear of being bathed (especially by her father), fear of going to the toilet, aggressive behaviour, a degree of self-injurious behaviour (hitting and punching herself), bed-wetting, increased clinginess to her mother and chronic urinary infections. Together, all these indicators gave a picture of high risk, which was later confirmed by her verbal disclosure and the medical evidence.

If sexual abuse is suspected and reported to the statutory child protection agencies, the child is likely to be given a formal interview. Often the clear disclosures made to primary caregivers are not repeated to the formal investigators. This was the case for Evelyn, the little girl who disclosed to the nursery worker. Even with such a clear disclosure, i.e. 'Daddy fuck my bum', investigators would need to know who daddy was (bearing in mind that some children have more than one daddy), what "fuck" meant to this child, and where she thought her bum was.

Children in this age range are likely to use idiosyncratic words to describe private parts. A primary caregiver is likely to know what the words are. Norleen and Heston's mother, for example, confirmed that "ting-a-ling" was the word used in their family for penis. Young children may also use metaphors like "snake" or "stick" for penis, or not possess the proper word for genitals. However, they are often very clear with gestures and pointing to the part of their body, or someone else's body, that they are referring to. This is, in part, why dolls with genitals are sometimes used in interviews with children in this age range. They act as an aid to discussion about touching.

> **We had, like, dolls and everything and you had to show what they did. I didn't actually want to show them but, like, I thought it's a better way – like using dolls, than just speaking it – 'cause say there was a bit you wouldn't – you didn't want to say – you could, like, show it instead.**
> *Natasha*

Some investigators have voiced concerns that anatomical dolls are suggestive to children, causing them to verbalise or indicate that something sexual has taken place when it has not.[2] These concerns have been so strongly expressed that subsequent government

---

2   In the original edition of *The Protectors' Handbook*, the following note regarding anatomical dolls was made. 'The use of "anatomically correct" dolls has been the subject of much debate. "Anatomically correct" is a misnomer; the dolls, for instance, have no ears. The female genitals have no clitoris. The dolls are no longer used in investigative interviews following guidance from the government on how to interview children (Home Office, 1992, replaced by 2002).

guidance on interviewing children has led to the dolls not being used in formal interviews. In my clinical experience, children will use what is available to them to explain what has happened to them, from attempting sexual demonstrations in the room to using their own toys and dolls. This is not in an investigative context. Additionally, spontaneous comments children make can add weight to suspicions of sexual abuse that are being investigated formally. This is shown in the example below, taken from an interview with a four-year-old.

Following the naming of private parts and a general discussion regarding who can and cannot touch children's private parts, the child begins to discuss the allegation of sexual abuse.

> Q: Has anyone ever touched your mary?
> Bonnie: Daddy has.

> Q: Daddy has. Can you show me on the little dolly, how Daddy touched you?
> Bonnie: He went like that. [Demonstrates with hand over vagina.]

> Q: When Daddy touched your mary, was that a good touch or a bad touch?
> Bonnie: A hurt touch.

> Q: A hurt touch.
> Bonnie: And it stinged.

Although the beginning of this sequence starts with a "leading" question (i.e. a question that suggests something has happened), the prior context allowed for benign genital contact to have occurred between parent and child. The child had shown some confusion about who is and is not allowed to touch private parts. This is developmentally appropriate, as children in this age range still may have adults helping them with toileting. It is interesting, though, that the child names "daddy" as the person who touches her private parts rather than mummy, who would, for the most part, be the parent involved in toileting. In response to the multiple choice question about good or bad touching, the child provided her own choices: a hurting touch, and it 'stinged'. This is very significant because neither of these answers was suggested by the interviewer, and they suggest some distress on the child's part regarding the touching. However, it is still not conclusively indicative of sexual abuse because it is possible that the hurting and stinging could be a result of, for example, an episode of diarrhoea.

> *Q: Did you tell anyone when Daddy touched you and hurt you?*
> *Bonnie: I told Aunt Cathy and Mummy. I won't let him do it again.*

> *Q: Did Daddy tell you not to say anything?*
> *Bonnie: Yup. He said, 'You don't tell anyone or if you do you're not coming to my house any more. Or nanny's house.' [Bonnie's parents were separated.] Don't tell him.*

> *Q: Don't tell him?*
> *Bonnie: 'Cause he thinks he didn't do it.*

> *Q: He thinks he didn't do it.*
> *Bonnie: But he did…*

> *Q: But he did . . .*
> *Bonnie: I didn't do anything naughty.*

> *Q: And you didn't do anything naughty.*
> *Bonnie: No . . . he's just fibbing.*

> *Q: He's just fibbing, is he?*
> *Bonnie: Don't tell him the bits I said. You just say, 'Why did you do that to Bonnie?'*

> *Q: I must ask him why he did that to you?*

Bonnie: Write this down. [Child gives interviewer a pencil and starts to dictate a message to Daddy.] To say – you smack his face and then get out.

Q: Smack his face?
Bonnie: Yes, 'cause he's naughty. [The child then begins to play out giving Daddy her message. She draws a picture of Daddy's house.] And here's a bell. It goes ring. Ring ring.

Q: Who's going to answer the door?
Bonnie: Daddy or Joan [Daddy's new partner]. And you say, 'Look at this message'.

Q: What is the message?
Bonnie: I'll say . . . you say . . . well, it's from Bonnie and she wants it for you and don't hang up.

Q: This is not for hanging up.
Bonnie: And then after . . . if he takes a seat you take a seat. When he says . . . when you want to go, you go . . . you say 'You're naughty 'cause you done that to Bonnie . . . ' Just stand there on the step [i.e. don't go in the house]. Just say to him, 'This is for you and you don't come and see Bonnie'. And when you've finished with it, come over to my house and give it to me.

This long and detailed transcript gives a flavour of the kind of information children in this age range give in formal interviews. There is not a lot of specific detail regarding the allegation itself. This partial transcript in and of itself is not sufficient to feel confident that a crime has been committed. But together with additional supporting information about her behaviour, the details of what she told Aunt Cathy and some of the qualitative material in her formal interview, there is a high likelihood that her father sexually abused her.

This interview also shows that the child's primary preoccupations are not with what has happened but what will happen in the future. Hence the urgency regarding the message to daddy. This is a very common preoccupation for children.

Here is another example from Heston and Norleen's interview. The little boy (Heston) is six years old and has Down's Syndrome. His sister (Norleen) is three. Heston has just hurt his finger in the door.

> *Q: Does it hurt?*
> Heston: How did I do it?
>
> *Q: You caught it in the door.*
> Heston: Silly.
>
> *Q: Was that silly?*
> Heston: Yes!
>
> *Q: Anywhere else hurts?*
> Heston: [Pointing at the doll's penis] That . . . ting-a-ling. It hurts. Look [touching the doll's penis] – hurts.
>
> *Q: Oh, dear. Who hurts your ting-a-ling?*
> Heston: Daddy.
>
> *Q: Your daddy does.*
> Heston: Yes! Him touch her bottom [pointing to his sister].
>
> *Q: Daddy touches Norleen's bottom.*
> Norleen: Yes [very quietly and turning away].
>
> *Q: Show me on the doll what he does.*
> Norleen: Daddy touch my bottom. [Norleen places her hand over vagina of small doll; puts her finger in vagina of doll.]
>
> *Q: Did you like what he did?*
> Norleen: No. It hurt. Daddy hurt my bottom.

When these children saw their father for a supervised court-ordered contact visit, they repeated their allegations to him. Heston immediately pointed to his father's genitals and started shouting, 'Bite it, bite it'. Norleen was very defiant and directly confronted her father, saying, 'You hurt my bottom. You are a naughty piggy.' During a game, both children had father lie down on the floor whilst they at first playfully hit him. Norleen said, 'I am going to make you bleed like Jesus'. (It was soon to be Easter.) She began hitting her father tentatively with a soft toy, changed to her shoe and then started to use her fists, slowly working from his feet until she delivered a vicious punch to his genitals.

Again, the amount of verbal material alone would not be considered sufficient to draw a conclusion. However, coupled with additional material, as well as the children's emotional response to the supervised contact session, there is a strong likelihood that sexual abuse had occurred.

Children in this age range provide a very limited amount of detail in formal interview settings. Primary caregivers usually can give much more information regarding the child's concerns and their behaviours.

5 to 12 age group

This is a wide age span. However, children in this age range will know right from wrong, and will be able to understand about secrets and threats. Clearly, there will be many of the same indicators as in the previous age group but the older age range leads to slightly different presentations.

Any verbal indication that sexual abuse is happening constitutes a red alert sign, and should be taken very seriously. It is very unlikely that children make up allegations of sexual abuse.

Children in this age range frequently tell other children rather than adults. Research indicates that children living at home are most likely to share worries with their best friends and parents, with mothers being very significant. There is a gender difference, with girls being twice as likely as boys to tell their best friends and mothers (Hallett *et al*, 2003, p 128). This is important for foster carers, as it is possible – and perhaps likely – that a foster child will disclose information to other children in the placement before telling an adult. It is important for foster carers to prepare their own children for this and make sure they know they should tell their parents.

In a study on the prevalence of sexual abuse, Kelly *et al* found that 50 per cent of their sample who disclosed sexual abuse told either a relative or a close friend (Kelly *et al*, 1991). In a more recent study (Cawson *et al*, 2000, p 83), 72 per cent of the children involved did not tell anyone about the sexual abuse when it was happening. Some told later, but almost a third still had not told anyone about their experience of sexual abuse by the time of the study. Often adults find out because the confidant tells a teacher or their parent. It is important that indirect or third-party disclosures are followed up by an adult and that someone speaks to the child who has been sexually abused. It would probably be helpful to have the confidant present when you talk to the child if this is practical. Repeated disclosures to a number of adults, or over a period of time, should be given weight.

Children in this age range clearly give more detail in their disclosures, although they can also use grown-up words incorrectly. For example, one young girl told her mother she had had sexual intercourse with a friend's father when she was staying overnight. Medical examination revealed she had not been penetrated and was still a *virgo intacta*. When questioned more closely by her mother, and asked to describe what had taken place, she stated clearly, 'He put his penis between my legs and moved it up and down.' She believed this to be sexual intercourse.

Children in this age range can also describe their experience metaphorically. They may say, for example, that they have been

stabbed. Whilst it is important to check that this is not the case, it is
equally important not to be too preoccupied with the literal
description (i.e. if there is no knife, then the disclosure is wholly
untrue).

These children can use many different ways of disclosing indirectly.
They may tell obliquely by referring to a friend who has a problem
or by writing about it in creative projects at school. Such fictional
accounts need to be taken seriously. The child or young person may
be testing the water regarding adult reactions to what is being said
or hinted at. They are asking for information about what might
happen as a result of disclosure. It is important for adults to know
the possible procedures if sexual abuse is disclosed. If you work with
children, you should also be sure that you are aware of policies and
procedures at your workplace should a child disclose any kind of
abuse to you.

Children frequently want adults whom they turn to for help to keep
the sexual abuse secret. You will have to decide if this is something
you can do. If you are in a professional role in relation to a child,
you would almost certainly be advised to inform the statutory child
protection workers. If you are a friend of the family or a parent, it is
important for you to remember that secrecy rarely protects. You
should share your concern with another trusted adult and together
plan what you are going to do.

Many protectors think that confronting the alleged perpetrator is
the best way to intervene. This is unlikely to help unless you have
already told others who will support you in your confrontation. If
the only person you tell is the alleged perpetrator, you can
inadvertently increase the risk for the child because you will have
alerted him to the child's attempt to get help. It is much better to
tell someone who will believe what the child has said and support
you in protecting the child from any further abuse.

Physical signs are harder to detect in children in this age range without
a specific medical examination, because adults have much less benign

contact with older children's private parts. Injuries and/or infections can easily be missed. If they *are* noticed, or a child complains about being sore, this should be followed up. There may be a benign explanation for it, but it is important to consider sexual abuse as a possible explanation in the absence of a credible alternative.

For young girls at the top end of this age range, becoming pregnant as a consequence of sexual abuse is a possibility. Many adults do not consider pregnancy in this age range so it can go undetected until it has progressed considerably, often committing the girl to giving birth. It is important to recognise that any pregnancy in this age range is irrefutable proof that a criminal offence has taken place. Advanced technology makes it possible to prove beyond a shadow of doubt who the father of the child is or is not. To test the DNA from an individual, consent from that individual is required.[3]

Sexualised behaviour and compulsive masturbation are, however, more common than pregnancy in this age range. At this age most children will have learned about what is considered appropriate behaviour, so inappropriately sexualised or masturbatory behaviour is a particularly strong sign of sexual abuse. Sexual overtures are unmistakable, with children making specific requests for sexual contact from adults or from other children. If the child has been sexually abused from a young age, she or he may still not really understand what is wrong with sexual activity, and may also have begun to see sexual contact as the way to negotiate life.

For older children who have not been abused from a young age, sexualised behaviour is less likely to occur until they reach the top end of this age range, where there is a developmental increase in sexual awareness anyway. Odd signals about sexual knowledge should be taken seriously at this age. It is difficult for children who have experienced sexual abuse to assess what they should or should

3   See, for example, www.homeoffice.gov.uk/science-research/using-science/dna-database/ for a more detailed discussion of DNA profiles being used in crime detection. The website indicates that DNA samples obtained for analysis from the collection of DNA at crime scenes and from samples taken from individuals in police custody can be held on the National DNA Database. DNA testing in paternity cases can only be done with consent.

not know, and making a judgement about what constitutes common knowledge regarding sex and sexual contact is likely to be problematic for them. So, for example, they can assume that everyone has sex with their father or brother; they may provide details about hardcore pornography without realising that this is not common knowledge; they may discuss sex with multiple partners, including being involved in group activities. All of these examples have arisen in my clinical practice. For the young person involved, this level of sexual activity can seem like the natural consequences of multiple sexually abusive experiences. They can easily be led into sexually exploitative experiences.[4]

Children who draw attention to their genitals by exposing themselves are also indicating to adults that this part of their body is overly important. All children know they have genitals; only a small minority think they should display them to others. Most will feel appropriately private about their bodies. Often the "flashing" is done in contexts where adult supervision is absent or diffuse, for example, at playtime at school. Adults hear about it because other children complain, or because it becomes the focus of attention. Often adults ignore the behaviour itself and try to distract other children. Whilst this may be appropriate at the time, it is important that it is followed up sensitively, both with the child and with the child's primary caregivers.

It can be difficult to assess what constitutes inappropriate sexual knowledge for this age range. At this age, children naturally become more aware of aspects of reproduction, for instance. Information about how the baby gets into and out of "mummy's tummy" become more the focus, and this is, of course, not an indicator of sexual abuse. It can be helpful, therefore, to be conscious of how much sexual information is likely to have reached the children with whom you are in contact. Some knowledge will have come from the family, so it is easy to have a sense of how much knowledge is

---

4   Barnardo's runs 29 Sexual Exploitation Projects in the UK. See www.barnardos.org.uk/ what_we_do/working_with_children_and_young_people/sexual_exploitation.htm for more information on the work they do in this area.

passed on in this way. Children will also be talking about sex with their friends and possibly receiving some education in school on the facts of life.

Most parents do not give explicit sexual information to their children, and what children are likely to receive from friends or school is quite predictable. Clearly, a child who describes a variety of sexual acts has developmentally inappropriate sexual knowledge. If this is coupled with experiential knowledge, such as, for example, texture, taste and smell, this is likely to be evidence of sexual experience that constitutes abuse. In the absence of the experiential knowledge, it is possible that a child may have received their information from pornographic films. But an accidental viewing is unlikely to result in a conversational knowledge of sexual activities; and if a child has been deliberately exposed to pornographic films, then this constitutes non-contact sexual abuse.

Children in this age range who are being sexually abused may be feeling helpless and trapped. If they dare not tell an adult what is happening, then they have to learn to live with the abuse until they are old enough to escape from it themselves. This process is described by Roland Summit as "the accommodation syndrome",[5] as a consequence of which children can, and do, develop intense feelings of despair that can be difficult to articulate (1983).

> I just – when he was doing it to me I just lost all communication. I didn't talk to him – I just wanted him to leave me alone.
> *Alison*

> I didn't really want to show it 'cause, like, I didn't want anyone to know – I was scared for anyone to know.
> *Natasha*

---

5   This is an old paper now but clinically still useful. It reminds us that retraction is part of the process and doesn't mean we shouldn't believe the first disclosure. It also points to the strange phenomenon that we disbelieve disclosures but believe retractions.

Such children can't speak out, and protecting adults must be prepared to look for other signs, such as behavioural disturbances. Sometimes a child will attempt suicide, but this can be easy for the adult to miss, often because the attempts are unsuccessful and do not resemble adult attempts. Children in this age range will often try to kill themselves by doing expressly what they have been told not to do. For example, they may cross the road unsafely, or take things that are locked away because they are dangerous, like bleach. They may take tablets but often the tablets taken would not kill and consequently the adults around them do not recognise the overdose as a suicide attempt. They may try to drown or smother themselves. They may do very dangerous and reckless things. In the next age range, their attempts to kill themselves are usually more recognisable, but that can be because the suicide attempts began in *this* age range, and their technique has become more deadly as they have grown older.

Equally, children in this age range may begin to run away. When they are very young, adults can consider this to be simply wandering off. But home should be where children run to; if they do not, adults should begin to ask why.

Often alcohol and drug use starts in this age range. Frequently, it is the perpetrator who introduces the child to alcohol or drugs. They do this to make it easier to persuade the child to do as they ask, as well as increasing the child's dependence on them. One ten-year-old girl, Tina, described her experience with hard drugs very clearly: 'First it was drugs and then "rudies", then it was "rudies" before drugs.' She drew a picture depicting the "before" and "after" feelings from drugs, describing the drugged experience as producing a lift or "floaty" feeling. Children can find that such substances provide a means of escaping, forgetting or self-medicating for their painful, disturbing and confusing experiences of sexual abuse.

> I started drinking when I was 11 with Martini, always out of the bottle, then I went on to Bacardi and vodka when I was 13 . . . alcohol was my only escape. It solved

> everything. I couldn't feel anything and nothing
> registered to my mind or my body. I drank in the
> morning, in the afternoon quite a lot, but mostly in the
> evenings at the pub or in the car.
> *Lisa*

So, drug and alcohol use can be indicators of abuse in this age
range, and protectors should always consider this as a possibility
when discovering a child is using these substances.[6]

Unexplained large sums of money and gifts should also make
protectors wary, especially if they are given directly to the child
without parental knowledge. These gifts can act as bribes and/or
"hush money" for keeping the inappropriate sexual contact secret.
Many sexual offenders give gifts to the child's caregiver. They might
offer to babysit, take the children on holidays or do some other
unsupervised activities that do not include the primary caregiver.
Some offenders deliberately target those living below the poverty
line, where such offers can be even more difficult to turn down and
can seem very helpful at the time.

Children often understand the role that gifts to their parents play in
the sexually abusive experiences. They recognise the often very real
difference this makes to the family's overall standard of living, and
the fact that such gifts make the sexual offender seem a paragon of
virtue.

The behaviours described above constitute red alert signs for this
age group. The most likely explanation is that sexual abuse is
occurring, especially if there are a number of these signs which are
noticed. The perpetrator is less likely to be a family member, as
children in this age range have greater mobility. But the younger the
child, the more likely it is that the perpetrator will be a member of
the child's family network.

---

6   High levels of alcohol misuse are reported for people with abusive pasts. See also
    Moncrief and Farmer (1998). See www.alcoholconcern.org.uk/files/20040709
    _145809_ptsd%20factsheet.pdf for a more detailed discussion of the impact of PTSD
    on alcohol misuse.

Other serious behavioural disturbances that may be related to experiences of sexual abuse are: hysterical symptoms (where the child seems to have a physical inability that has no medical cause, such as blindness or paralysis); anorexia and other eating disorders (Oppenheimer et al, 1985);[7] bed-wetting, especially if the young person has previously been dry; soiling and messing with poo; obsessional washing and cleaning; night terrors or sleep problems, especially if these have not been a continuous feature of the child's development; hurting animals; fire setting; or glue sniffing or extreme alcohol and drug use.

Clearly, sexual abuse is not the only explanation for these behavioural disturbances. However, it is important to remember that a child is communicating something by their behaviour. It can be useful to ask yourself, as a possible protector, what is this child trying to tell me by their behaviour that they cannot tell me in words?

> ### Q: Do you think there might have been any signs or clues that you were being sexually abused before you told?
> **Alison:** My behaviour at school. The teacher just said that sometimes he felt like just taking me and shaking me. My mum just put it down to – 'cause she was pregnant with my sister – that she just thought it was jealousy. I just weren't doing nothing – sitting there, and if he told me to do my work I'd just look at him. My behaviour round the other children as well – I didn't want to play with them, didn't want to go near them. And what made it worse, my teacher was a man, and I just – I'd just, like, sit in the corner and isolate myself from the rest of the class. So he told my mum. He just called my mum up and my mum said they came to the decision that it was because of my little sister. They should have asked me.

---

7   Childhood sexual abuse increases the risks of women developing eating disorders – and can even impact on their children – see http://news.bbc.co.uk/1/hi/health/4417938.stm.

I weren't as open as what I used to be – um, I was always sort of – hanging round her – if he come down – I was hanging round her – I didn't want to go out with him or nothing. Um – and when my sister was born I always used to try and make sure my mum was next to her, not him. I didn't want him going near her.

I used to scream at my little sister – towards my mum as well – she'd tell me to do something – I was standing there, like, you know – 'No, I'm not doing it. Do it yourself.' I started to blame her as well for not finding out what was going on.

Natasha: *You can tell by, like, the way they act – 'cause like some of them might be petrified of men, so, like, they won't go near that man . . . you might have, like, acted different – you might have had nightmares, and dreams – some people wet the bed and everything.*

Their education might, like, drop because they'll be scared of it and they might not want to eat, they might be sick, and 'I don't want to do this, I don't want to do that', they might stay in, they might stay in their bedroom, they might always want to be out – like, lots of things could be hints.

Q: Do you think you did any of these things?
Natasha: *Yeah I did – dreams, wet the bed, everything.*

Q: Did your mum notice these, do you think?
Natasha: *If she noticed them I don't think she did anything, or like, whether it was like 'I can't be bothered'.*

Some behaviours are very directly linked to the abuse. For example, if a child is regularly and repeatedly buggered by an abuser, then it is not surprising that the child soils and messes themselves. Similarly, a child who is orally raped may develop an eating disorder.

Protectors need to recognise that there is a reason why a child behaves in the ways listed above. It is important to find out why these behaviours are happening, especially if commonsense approaches do not bring the behaviour under control. Asking about unwanted sexual experiences, especially if a child is clearly conveying distress through their behaviour, is extremely important. By guessing or discovering the clues, the adult relieves the child of both the burden of telling and the guilt for disobeying the injunction not to tell.

12 to 16 age group

Sixteen is an arbitrary cut-off point but it is used because it coincides with the law regarding the age of consent for heterosexual activity. Under this age, sexual intercourse is not sanctioned by the law, and constitutes a sexual offence.[8] Consequently, pregnancy, terminations and venereal diseases in this age range all indicate that a crime has been committed. They don't necessarily indicate abuse in the sense of non-consenting sexual intercourse, but it is a possibility that sexual abuse has taken place if a young woman under 16 becomes pregnant or has a venereal disease.

Many young people who have been sexually abused become more sexually active than their peers. The Adverse Childhood Experiences Study [9] found a graded relationship between the number of categories of adverse childhood experiences and each of the adult health risk behaviours and diseases that they studied. One of these related to the number of sexual partners. This is likely to have a huge impact on reproductive health. It almost certainly increases the chances of cervical cancer and sexually transmitted diseases, including HIV, and also compromises fertility. Sexual activity can be a coping mechanism for surviving sexual abuse. For young women, there is the fear that they will conceive a child from the perpetrator.

---

8   www.opsi.gov.uk/acts/acts2003/ukpga_20030042_en_1. This details the Sexual
     Offences Act 2003, including offences against children.

9   www.acestudy.org/.

By having sex with many men, the paternity of the child will be in doubt, and this may make the child easier to parent. This strategy – which may sound extreme to some – is frequently employed and described by young women. I have been involved in a number of court cases where DNA testing has been sought to confirm a child's paternity. Often the shortlist for paternity involves family members including brothers and fathers simultaneously. Sometimes, despite numerous tests, paternity remains unknown, indicating that the biological father is not from the shortlist supplied. This suggests a high level of sexual activity with multiple partners, possibly including family members.

Young people in this age range may decide they want to tell about the sexual abuse, and do so. Others blurt it out in a moment of weakness or anger. Or, they may make oblique reference to a past experience of sexual abuse in a vague or ambiguous way. For example, one young man hinted to his residential worker that he had previously been sexually abused. Correctly, the worker followed up the hints. During the investigation, the young man gave details with little prompting. He had clearly made a decision to tell.

> *Q: You know when you talked the other night to your keyworker about friends?*
> *Keith: Yes.*

> *Q: Could you tell us a bit more about it?*
> *Keith: I don't want to get him in trouble and lose his job – he's single and needs the money.*

> *Q: Do you think you could tell us what happened?*
> *Keith: Well, I woke up in the night, and I wanted a pill. I forget what for now. I knocked on the sleeping-in room. I remember it was one o'clock. Anyway, I knocked on the door and he opened it and asked what I needed. I asked for a pill. He gave me a pill, then said, 'There is no point in going back to bed now, you might as well come back to bed with me'.*

I didn't really know what was going on . . . he came to hug me from behind and . . . well . . . he did the business.

Q: What do you mean by "the business"?
Keith: *Well, he bummed me.*

This example shows some of the characteristics of disclosure for a young person of this age. He had decided to tell. After some hesitancy, he begins to tell of his experience. He remembers details from the experience, such as the time in the morning, whilst at the same time he employs euphemisms to describe his experience. Where a younger child might use metaphor, an older child uses euphemism – in this case "the business". Both are ways of distancing oneself from the reality of the experience, especially the feelings that go with it.

Clearly, if a young person has not made a decision to tell, and the experience of sexual abuse is disclosed accidentally, the likelihood of retracting or taking it back is greater. However, some young people experience pressure from their families to retract, or feel so lonely and isolated when they are away from their families that they are prepared to say it did not happen, even if it did. If a young person retracts, protectors should not consider the original allegations to have no substance.

There are situations where young women repeatedly make allegations to the police, often about assaults by strangers, which, when investigated, are found to be untrue. In many of these cases, the young woman has been previously sexually abused and has either not disclosed it or has not been believed. Although the current details may not be true, the disclosure of sexual abuse is essentially true. This is very serious and needs to be dealt with, as it not only undermines the credibility of the young woman herself, but also of all women who report sexual crimes to the police. Often the young woman will eventually disclose her earlier experience of sexual abuse, but in such instances she is much less likely to be believed.

These issues are raised as indicators of sexual abuse because they are part of the more complex disclosing process in this age range. Retractions and false allegations of sexual crimes are both very unusual. They are most likely to occur in young people who have been sexually abused but who are not yet ready to be clear about their experiences or the identity of the perpetrator.

Young people of this age who have been sexually abused may be experiencing a range of distressing and disturbing behaviours. They can take some of their feelings out on others (externalising), or take them out on themselves (internalising). Often there is a gender difference, with boys usually externalising and girls internalising. Sexual offending behaviour against other children becomes much more apparent in this age range. If any child or young person is involved in sexually aggressive behaviour (including committing actual sexual offences), it is important that protectors consider that the juvenile perpetrator and sexual bully has been, or currently still is, a victim of another perpetrator (usually an adult). This does not excuse their current behaviour but should alert protectors to look for an adult who has encouraged, and perhaps taught, the young person to behave in such ways. Many convicted adult male sexual offenders describe beginning their careers as sexual offenders at 13 or 14 years of age after themselves being victims of sexual abuse.

Many sexually abused young women in this age group become involved in prostitution. In the video, *Incest: A crime of violence*, one young woman described prostitution as her way of gaining control over her experience (Droisen, 1986). She had been sexually abused and now she had sexual control of her male clients. But she also recognised that the men had the money to buy her if they chose to, and that therefore the sense of control was false. As well as gaining a sense of control, abused young women may also have to turn to prostitution to earn money to support alcohol and drug addictions arising from sexual abuse.

Young people who have been sexually abused over long periods of time do not view sexual contact as a way of expressing love and emotional intimacy. Instead, sexual contact can be seen as a means of expressing power and control (Saradjian, 1996).[10] High levels of sexual activity, with or without the exchange of money, are a strong indication that sexual abuse may have occurred.

It is possible for a young person who has been sexually abused to become addicted to the heightened arousal the abusive experience produces. They can then feel a physiological need to have sexual contact divorced from any emotional closeness. The young person is also likely to be confused about their physical feelings and may not label or recognise their sexual feelings as sexual, or may mistakenly label anxiety and fear as sexual feelings.

There are also gender differences in relation to what is considered appropriate sexual activity for this age range, with boys given more freedom for sexual exploration with girls, than vice versa. Being treated and used as a sexual object by other people is extremely damaging. Many young people take their angry feelings out on themselves by mutilating and hurting themselves physically.

> I used to, and sometimes still do, cut myself when I am frustrated, angry or upset because of what happened. When I am frustrated it lets the tension out to see the blood. When I feel guilty about what happened and scared that it will happen again, I cut myself so I am uglier and so it doesn't happen again. I cut myself when I am not sure how to cope with my anger. I can never direct my anger at the appropriate person so I cut myself . . . Cutting is a sort of release – it's like taking all the bad out of your body, all the crap that's been left behind for me to deal with.
> *Lisa*

---

10 Jacqui Saradjian designed a questionnaire, "What sex means", which coded responses into seven categories: positive physical feelings, negative feelings, bonding, emotional warmth, give pleasure, own pleasure, power and control. It can be used with young people.

Self-harm happens in the younger age range, but most frequently comes to adult attention in this older age range. It is important to differentiate between self-inflicted cuts meant to kill and those meant to injure and hurt: they are conveying different messages (Smith *et al*, 1998). Cuts to harm are generally made on such parts of the body as the arms, legs, face, stomach or back. They are not directed at arterial points which, if cut, could result in bleeding to death.

Suicide attempts in this age range more closely resemble adult attempts (and it can often be in the context of recovering from a suicide attempt that a young person discloses sexual abuse for the first time).

Equally serious are breakdowns, where a young person cuts him or herself off from the outside world, remaining mute or suffering from a serious psychiatric disorder. These consequences are often signs that the young person has suffered a severe trauma, such as a violent rape or protracted undiscovered sexual abuse.

Many of the serious problems discussed in the previous section are also relevant for this age group. Mental health practitioners and adult caregivers need to ask why a child or young person is behaving in a disturbed way. Neither children nor adults behave in this fashion for no reason. The older a child gets, the easier it can be to concentrate on what the child is doing rather than why the child is doing it. It is crucial to ask why at every age. Many factors could be responsible, such as death in the family or severe marital disharmony, but the possibility of sexual abuse should never be ignored. Additionally, some disturbed behaviours can mean the young person is continuing to experience abuses and traumas in addition to the original one.

Children who have already experienced sexual abuse are more vulnerable to other sexual offenders, especially if the original abuse remains undisclosed. Many of the behaviours they display can increase their vulnerability. If they are drunk or drugged, they will not be able to protect themselves. If they are on the run or sleeping rough, they may be raped or sexually exploited in exchange for a safe place to sleep for the night. These are all additional abuses that will make recovery more difficult. If you are involved with a young person who is engaged in high-risk behaviours, it is important not to blame them completely for what has happened, but to recognise what has driven them to such extremes. Many young people in this age range will have been abused over a number of years and as a consequence will have learned to live with sexual abuse as an inevitable reality in their lives, especially if they are sexually abused by more than one person.

It is also essential to ensure that, as time passes, an episode of known sexual abuse is not forgotten or seen as irrelevant to the difficulties the young person may have later in life. This often happens, especially with adult survivors who are presently in mental health facilities. Their current problems are often construed as being disconnected from experiences of childhood sexual abuse.

This age range has more green indicators because the number of possible explanations for distressing behaviours is much greater. Some of the green indicators may have appeared in the red alert section in a younger age range – pregnancy being an example. In trying to assess the weight of any one indicator, it is vital to consider a range of explanations, including sexual abuse. If another explanation seems to fit the current difficulties and there is some improvement following a tackling of the alternative reason, then that explanation may be correct. However, if a number of explanations have been used and lots of interventions have been tried, and yet challenging behaviours continue, it may be that adults have not considered sexual abuse.

It can be very frustrating if you suspect abuse, but the young person will neither confirm nor refute your suspicion. In these cases, it can be helpful to discuss protection issues, to be clear that the young person's safety is important to you, and that you want to help them feel confident and secure in who they are and where they are going.

Following up your concerns

When using the list of indicators, it can be helpful to talk over your observations or concerns with another adult you trust. Many protectors correctly identify indicators but often play down or dismiss their significance. Then, with the hindsight a disclosure gives, the indicators are remembered clearly.

Alison's teacher and mother thought something was not right but they convinced themselves that it was to do with Alison's jealousy of her younger sister. Of course, once her mother knew what was wrong, a host of other odd incidents fell into place.

If you are seriously concerned about a child or young person you know, and they have not disclosed clearly to you, it can be helpful to record your observations in a diary. Try to describe accurately what you saw, use the child's words if they tell you something, note anything you thought odd or unusual. If you discuss your concerns with someone else, especially with a professional, make sure they record both your concerns and their advice to you (especially if they tell you not to worry and it later transpires you should have). A single episode of distressing behaviour (unless it involves an unambiguous disclosure or a genital injury) is rarely a cause for concern. It is important that you trust your judgement and your knowledge of the child or young person. Noticing children's behaviour and acting on "funny feelings" is part of protecting children.

SIGNS AND INDICATORS OF CHILD SEXUAL ABUSE

Under 5s

RED

Disclosure
Genital injuries
VD
Vivid details of sexual activity (such
as penetration,oral sex, ejaculation)
Compulsive masturbation
(contextually abnormal)
Sexual drawings
Sexualised play usually acting out
explicit sexual acts

GREEN

Person specific fear
Nightmares
Chronic urinary/vaginal infections
Soreness of genitals/bottom
Situationally specific fears
Fear of being bathed
Fear of being changed
Fear of being put to bed

BLUE

Developmental regression
Hostile/aggressive behaviour
Psychosomatic condition

5–12 years

RED

Disclosure
Genital injuries
VD
Sexual stories/poems
Sexual drawings
Exposing themselves
Masturbation in contextually
inappropriate fashion
Promiscuity
Suicide attempts
Running away
Alcohol and drug abuse

GREEN

Arson
Soreness of genitals/bottom
Chronic urinary/vaginal infections
Obsessional washing
Depression
Hysterical symptoms
Enuresis
Encopresis
Anorexia
Glue sniffing
Nightmares
Truanting
Unexplained large sums of
money/gifts

BLUE

Abdominal pains
Developmental regression
Peer problems
Psychosomatic conditions
School problems

12+

RED

Disclosure
Genital injuries
Self-mutilation of breast/genitals
Pregnancy – under 14
VD – under 14
Prostitution

GREEN

Sexual boasting/stories/jokes
VD – over 14
Pregnancy – over 14
Sexual offending
Rebellious against men (specific gender)
Drug and alcohol abuse
Suicide attempts
Self-mutilation
Continual lying
Truanting
Running away
Hysterical symptoms
Obsessional washing
Psychotic episodes

BLUE

Depression
Anorexia
School refusing
Peer problems
Authority problems
Delinquency
Psychosomatic conditions

References

Cawson P, Wattam C, Brooker S and Kelly G (2000) *Child Maltreatment in the United Kingdom: A study of the prevalence of child abuse and neglect*, London: NSPCC

Droisen A, Producer (1987) *Incest: A crime of violence,* Iriscope Productions.

Hallett C, Murray C and Punch S (2003) 'Young people and welfare: negotiating pathways', in Hallett C and Prout A (eds) *Hearing the Voices of Children: Social policy for a new century*, London: Routledge

Hellett J and Simmonds J (2003) *Parenting a Child who has been Sexually Abused: A training programme for foster carers and adopters,* London: BAAF

Home Office (1992) *Memorandum of Good Practice on Video-Recorded Interviews with Child Witnesses for Criminal Proceedings*, London: HMSO

Home Office (2002) *Achieving Best Evidence in Criminal Proceedings: Guidance for vulnerable and intimidated witnesses, including children*, London: HMSO

Kelly L, Regan L and Burton S (1991) *An Exploratory Study of the Prevalence of Sexual Abuse in a Sample of 16–21-Year-Olds*, London: Child Abuse Studies Unit, PNL

Moncrief J and Farmer R (1998) 'Sexual abuse and the subsequent development of alcohol problems', *Alcohol and Alcoholism*, 33:6, pp 592–601.

Oppenheimer R, Howells K, Palmer RL and Chaloner DA (1985) 'Adverse sexual experience in childhood and clinical eating disorders;

a preliminary description', *Journal of Psychiatric Research*, 19, pp 357–61

Saradjian J (1996) *Women who Sexually Abuse Children: From research to clinical practice*, Chichester: Wiley

Smith G, Saradjian J and Cox D (1998) *Women and Self Harm*, London: The Womens' Press

Summit R (1983) 'The child sexual abuse accommodation syndrome', *Child Abuse & Neglect*, 7, pp 177–93

3

Reducing the risks and helping children to tell

This chapter deals with ways of reducing the risk of sexual abuse. It contains useful information to give children in advance of sexual abuse taking place; encourages you to consider ways of talking about concerns you might have about a child or young person; and discusses how you should deal with a child telling you about sexual abuse.

The adults most closely connected to children, their primary caregivers, have a greater impact on children's recovery than professionals alone. Only in a minority of cases do children need to talk about sexual abuse with professional helpers. A believing and supportive adult, especially a primary caregiver, makes all the difference for a good recovery from the experience of sexual abuse. Consequently, all protecting adults need skills in knowing how to talk about it, in case and preferably *before* it happens, following up your concerns, and feeling confident about what you might do if a child discloses sexual abuse to you. Good communication skills are essential. This involves being able not only to talk about sexual abuse but also to listen carefully, observe and comment on what you see and hear.

How to talk about sexual abuse

It is helpful to talk about sexual abuse with other adults first so that you can identify a network of support for yourself in case you have to help a child or someone you love recover from the experience. If helpers don't have anyone to talk to, they can begin to feel overburdened by the awfulness and unable sometimes to listen to any more details about sexual abuse. This can apply just as much to professional helpers as to caregivers. Also, if you cannot think of anyone you could talk to about something like this, it will be hard for you to convey the need for openness to your children. Children will recognise your difficulty and will try to protect you from their experience.

Many adults wonder when to begin giving their children information. Foster carers often feel constrained about raising the issue of sexual abuse with their foster child. This may be because it has not been confirmed by a finding in fact or a criminal conviction or they are waiting for the child to raise the issue spontaneously. Whilst it may seem best to wait until children ask, this can be a risky strategy. Children will assume that all adults are going to be safe and that what they do is always right. They are dependent on their primary caregivers to help them shape their understanding of the world. An experience in foster care is a wonderful opportunity to broaden a child's view about what family life is like and to encourage them to see adults, especially primary caregivers, as resources. It is an opportunity to correct misinformation and, in some cases, to begin to form healthy new attachments. So the earlier you start to talk to children, the better. The following are some issues you can discuss, even with very young children.

Keeping safe

When your child goes to school, the issue of "keeping safe" may be part of the school curriculum. All the research shows that, while parents may want schools to talk to their children about basic sex information and perhaps child safety programmes, children want their parents to talk to them about these issues. Additionally, the effects of these programmes are limited when only done in a school context. When parents also support and elaborate the messages given in school, the impact is much greater for the child and also develops along with them. It can help for you to know how the school will introduce the topics to your child, so you can reinforce the messages at home. If the school does not offer "keeping safe" as part of the curriculum, you should encourage them to do so. There are a number of safety programmes designed for use in schools.[1]

Body awareness

For the very young, or those who cannot articulate their experiences, it will be important to listen to them and observe their behaviour. These children are more likely to tell you things through showing you. Giving children a language to talk about their bodies is the first step. Most families have words for private parts and become involved in discussing toileting with small children before this becomes a private activity. Developing a language to talk about bodies is a good first step towards the more complex discussion about unwanted touching. For foster carers, giving a child the language used in your family can be helpful, as the child may not have words to describe their body and may have a very limited and distorted idea about how their body functions. This is especially true in cases of neglect.

It is important that foster carers watch how other adults and children interact with the foster child, and vice versa. Sometimes adults can be over-insistent on cuddles and kisses. If a child says no to unwanted hugs and kisses it is important not to insist that they accept them. If you do, you will be conveying the message that the child cannot make their own judgements about what is pleasurable

---

1   Kidscape, set up in 1985, now deals more with bullying, but when first set up its focus
     was child abuse. See www.kidscape.org.uk.

and what is not, and that they don't have the right to say no. You may find that your foster child makes inappropriate invitations to other children or adults. You may need to alert your kinship network to this and request feedback if it happens. You will need to be more vigilant during social situations until you feel confident that your family rules regarding privacy and safe touching have been learnt by your foster child.

If your child has a physical disability that means that regular physical contact by another is necessary, it is important that they are able to indicate what they like or dislike about other people's handling of them. Clearly verbal skills help, but children can also convey satisfaction or dissatisfaction with the way in which they are being handled non-verbally – for example, by crying out or pulling away when they don't like something.

Knowing your child's social network and surroundings

Part of protecting children is knowing where they are, who they are with, where they are going and what they are doing. Young children often have a very limited circle of friends, adult carers and places to go, but as a child moves away from the home into nursery school or playgroup, or to be with babysitters or childminders, it is important that you have enough information about the adult caregivers to whom you are entrusting your child's care. If your child is being looked after by someone else, how well do you know that person? Have you been clear to childminders about what you consider acceptable behaviour in relation to discipline, whether your child can be taken out and if so, under what conditions, and what other adults and children may they come into contact with? By discussing these matters with caregivers, you convey the message that you take the protection of your child seriously and that you want other adults to do so as well.

It is important to check with your child how their time away has been, not in an inquisitorial style but out of interest, and to reassure yourself they have been safe and secure. Making such discussions a normal part of life also lays down the foundation for the future, when much more autonomous behaviour is developmentally appropriate, such as children going to school on their own, going out with friends, or going on school trips.

You should also use the individual names of adult caregivers, rather than a general title like teacher. This ensures you and your child can be clear about who is being discussed.

Types of touching

It is important to talk to children and young people about appropriate and inappropriate touching. Such discussions can start at a young age and be adjusted as the child gets older. This is especially important in a fostering context where preparing your own children (or grandchildren) will help to form part of a protective network for the child arriving and for the children in your family network. Then if an incident of unwanted touching does occur, you will be more confident about how to talk about it. If you are used to the subject, you will also be able to convey the necessary under-reaction that allows children to carry on speaking about what has happened. It is better to deal with the incident, than to discover much later that more serious secret sexual touching has been going on for some time.

You may want to start talking about simple concepts like bad and good touching, which includes hitting, kicking, punching, biting and scratching, as well as kisses, cuddles, snuggles and hugs. As the child gets older, you should incorporate ideas about their body being their own, and encourage the child to develop a sense of privacy or body space. Children with severe physical disabilities will need to have this message modified. When foster children arrive, you will need to explain your family rules on this topic to them. In part you want them to understand that your family may be different to where they were before.

Children may enjoy playing with their genitals, often taking no notice of when or where they do so. It is important that they receive a message from parents and other caregivers about when and where they should enjoy the pleasures of their own bodies. If they continue to do so publicly they may be at risk, as this provides a perfect opening for someone wanting to sexually abuse children.

Similarly, young children can express an interest in touching or looking at adults' genitals, often in the context of going to the toilet or bathing. This can begin to feel uncomfortable and most caregivers will assert their right to privacy. Children can benefit from hearing their parents or foster carers model assertive behaviour in relation to touching. This helps children learn to both give and receive comments about touching. It is important that touch is seen as a two-way process – so if you (or anyone in your family) feel uncomfortable with some touching, this should be discussed. You may discuss it with another adult first, but it should be discussed with the child or young person.

An example of the above concerns a 15-year-old young man in a residential unit who was known to have been sexually abused in his family of origin. One morning, after repeatedly knocking on his bedroom door asking him to get up, a female member of staff opened the door and the boy jumped out of his bed naked, with no show of modesty. Given the numerous attempts to warn him that she was going to come in, including verbal prompts to get up, the boy's behaviour has to be viewed with some degree of suspicion. It is important it is addressed rather than ignored. Repeated occurrences suggest that more than just a simple mistake is involved. It may only involve female members of staff, who may keep quiet because they are embarrassed. In this case, the young lad had started to organise younger female residents to get him up in the morning. As adults, we need to be aware of the sexual ambiguity that is being expressed here. This demonstrates potential grooming by the young man. Additionally, he is minimising the role of adults as both caregivers (i.e. asking the female residents to look after him) and as external inhibitors (by setting up the younger female residents in disobeying the residential staff).

If you are clear about what you consider appropriate touching, and your child has experience of you giving feedback to other adults and children, they will be more likely to use you as a source of help if they have a problem with unwanted or confusing touching. Concentrating on touching is better than trying to identify potential abusers, as this focus offers the greatest protection, does not exempt anyone, and encourages children to judge each situation independently. In the example above involving a residential unit, where a number of children and young people with shared family of origin experiences are together, it is harder to expect other young people to comment on inappropriate requests. This situation can also arise in a foster family with many foster children or a sibling group. The children and young people, because of their own inappropriate experiences, may be less likely to raise issues of bullying or sexual touching with their foster carer. This is why it is so important for foster carers to prepare children (who may be their own, extended family's or foster children in the placement) for receiving a new foster child to the placement where touching may be a significant issue. The focus of this book is sexual abuse, but experiences of domestic violence and physical abuse are both likely to lead to confusion and anxiety about touching in family situations.

Secrets

Because many sexual offenders tell children to keep the abuse secret, you may want to think about how you would counteract this message or enable your child to be confident enough not to keep the secret. For foster children it can be helpful to distinguish between private, secret and confidential. As looked after children, these issues will have been played out through their exposure to the court system. They will understand about family loyalties and may be reluctant to talk about what happened at home. Many children have found that information they did not want disclosed to their birth parents was disclosed as part of the court process. The powerful combination of threats and the unknown outcome of proceedings is very silencing. Imagine what it would feel like to have your birth mother talk to you during contact about something you asked specifically to be kept from her.

Children under the age of three do not really understand what a secret is. For older children, you may want to encourage them to share their secrets with someone they trust. It may be useful to call some secrets "surprises" as a way of introducing nuance to the issue. By opening out the "secret debate", there can at least be an opportunity for someone else to know and to decide if it is a secret that should be kept. This may be very important as children grow up, as many children who have been sexually abused choose to tell another child first. This may mean your child is chosen as the confidant of another child. Having had the discussion about secrets within your family, you can be confident that you will be told about any situations involving confusing touching. If a child is at all unsure about keeping something secret, they should discuss it with another trusted person, preferably an adult. It can help to be clear that anything harmful should not be kept secret.

Encouraging children to tell

It is important that children know that you want them to tell you if another child or an adult is hurting or upsetting them in any way. There may be some situations that are confusing rather than clearly hurtful, and they need to be discussed as well. Bullying may be one such situation, although this is not the focus of this book.[2]

In the first instance, you want to give your child the message that it is all right to talk to grown-ups about issues that concern the child or young person. It is very important that they see adults and especially parental figures as sources of help. This will, in turn, influence the kind of parent they will become. You may also want to

---

2   For further information about bullying, see Kidscape at
     www.kidscape.org.uk/childrenteens/index.asp.

help them decide who in their current network they could trust and talk to other than yourself. The identification of a range of protecting adults for children to turn to is extremely important. Sometimes children mistakenly think their parents would not be able to deal with their difficulties. And sometimes they are right. For children in the care system, helping them understand why they are in care is an important task. This is likely to include the issue of their family of origin being unable to acknowledge or deal with sexual abuse satisfactorily. As a foster carer, you may have to think of reasons why this might be the case. This could include a parent's own history of being abused, which has compromised their ability to protect the next generation.

Rehearsal

You may want to encourage your child to think about what they might do if they were in certain hypothetical risk situations. These need not focus exclusively on sexual abuse. Parents or other primary caregivers could ask children what they would do if there was a fire alarm or if someone became very ill or hurt themselves very badly. This would make children more confident about dealing with risk situations in general so they would know whom to turn to and what to do if sexual abuse became an issue for them. It would also increase their problem-solving skills, a factor known to be correlated with psychological resilience.

Helping children to develop strategies for dealing with bullying, sexual and racial harassment and other forms of oppression is also very valuable, even for children who may not themselves be the target. With these strategies, a child observing an episode of bullying, for example, may feel more able to tell about it; and children will also be encouraged to protect one another. Also, being able to identify bullying or harassing types of behaviours will help children to recognise situations where hatred is allowed to flourish. Many siblings show survivor guilt when removed from situations where someone in the family was targeted. This may involve feelings of relief that they were not picked on or, indeed, feelings of shame that they felt compelled to participate in behaviours they knew or felt to be wrong.

Helping children and young people assess when it is safe enough to challenge and confront is extremely important. It is useful to explain that it is not the child's responsibility to change other people's prejudiced views, and that sometimes it is best to walk away from the situation rather than try to sort it out. This is especially true in situations involving domestic violence, which so often is the backdrop to other forms of child abuse.[3]

Using books and other resources

Having books and other appropriate material about sex education and sexual abuse, around the home, conveys an openness regarding both sexual knowledge in general, and sexual abuse in particular. Some children prefer to read about it rather than to talk directly to an adult. It might be useful to check what material is available at your local library. If there is nothing for children, young people or adults on protecting children from sexual abuse, you may like to make some suggestions and then check regularly that the material is still available.

> My old school, they had on a wall somewhere ChildLine and the phone number . . . the books about sexual abuse were only in the adult section . . . and like, you really had to look to find them. I once stumbled across this book [on sexual abuse], and, like, half the pages were missing. Someone had been ripping out pages and I was, like, trying to read it, and I was, like, "Help" [so] I took it to the librarian . . . and he goes, 'Oh, don't worry, most of the books are like that' – like he's not really worried.
> *Natasha*

---

3   For further information on domestic violence, see www.thehideout.org.uk.

Try to read or see the material first before giving it to your children. Some material is very explicit or may give messages you do not agree with or is promoting a view you do not share. If this is the case, you may find you cannot deal with the questions children ask. Much that is written or produced is not for all children. The material can be aimed at a particular age range or, more commonly, can assume that all children are white and able-bodied. While the internet now opens up a range of possibilities that are very empowering for children and young people, it does not replace conversation and discussion that underpin our most important source of psychological health – relationships. Indeed, many parents have no idea what their children are doing on the internet.[4]

Trying to address the issue of risk from close family members can be difficult. Using resources developed to help children and their caregivers talk about sexual abuse can make it easier as some of these books specifically mention family members. It is important to remember that the biggest risk to children still comes from people known to them, but it can be difficult to get this into perspective when the media regularly reports cases of child abductions. The case of Shannon Matthews, reported missing and then later found with an extended family member, is more typical than stranger abductions, which do occur but are very rare.[5]

You should use the intimate knowledge you have about your child to decide if short stories, colouring books, videos, internet sites or a combination of all of these materials would be the most effective way to *talk* about protecting your child from sexual abuse. A detailed list of useful organisations is provided in the Appendix.

---

4   Advice for parents on keeping their children safe while on the internet is available at www.kidsmart.org.uk/parents.

5   The murder of Sarah Evelyn Isobel Payne, abducted and killed by a stranger, Roy Whiting, is a high-profile example of the unusual case. Shannon Matthews disappeared on 19 February 2008. She was found on 14 March 2008 at her stepfather's uncle's home. Her mother has been implicated in her disappearance.

Following up your concerns

It is important that you follow up any concerns you have about children you care for or come into contact with. This can include concerns arising from your own observations or discussions with the child, even if it is not your own child. It can sometimes be easier for someone else to raise worries that the primary caregiver may have noticed but is not yet able to deal with.

You may notice children behaving sexually with one another. You will need to get the children to stop before you talk about it with them.

It may be obvious what the children were doing. It may seem harmless. On the whole, adults do not worry about incidents where children seem to be exploring physical differences. However, if the children have taken off their clothes, are putting things into each other's genitals or bottoms, or one child is clearly bullying another child into continuing, it is necessary for you to explain what is wrong about this kind of behaviour.

If the episode involves children from more than one family, it is important to share your concerns with the other primary caregivers. This should include not only what happened but also how you managed it, including what you said.

When children are involved in incidents with other children, it can be difficult to decide if their contact is sexually abusive, especially if the age difference is very small. These are some of the things that can help you to decide.

> – *Is there a significant age gap (five years or more), or a marked imbalance between the children in physical size or intellectual development?*

> – *Have any threats been used in the incident? Has there been any physical coercion?*

*– Are any of the children old enough to understand about
right and wrong? Have any of the children been specifically
told not to do this before?*

*– Has the episode been conducted in a secret, covert way?
Is there any evidence of premeditation – that one child had
decided in advance what they were going to do?*

*– Have there been past episodes with any of the
participants that might suggest a compulsive element to
the behaviour?*

*– Is any child involved in the behaviour connected to a
family where there are current safeguarding concerns?*

If the answer is yes to a number of these questions, it is important
that the caregivers follow up the incident with all the children
involved, separately, and with their primary caregivers if it involves
more than one family. This is especially important if there is a
significant age gap, if threats or overt coercion have been used, of if
there has been an element of premeditation. In these situations, it is
likely that one of the children may have been taught to behave in
this way by an adult. In my clinical practice, I have seen examples of
very young children involved in sexual games that were sexually
abusive and which made most of the children feel uncomfortable
yet constrained from telling their parents. I have also had a number
of cases of teenage girls involved in coercive sexual experiences with
peers where everyone minimised the psychological effects on the
young women involved. I have also had cases where young men
were targeted by older women, and adults failed to identify this as
sexually abusive (in her book on female sexual offending, Saradjian
describes some of the patterns involved (1996)).

If you feel uncomfortable about some touching you observe
between adults and children, it is important that you investigate and
do not pretend it did not happen, or that you misinterpreted it. It is
likely that in the course of a career of working with children you will

have come into contact with a colleague who has been inappropriate in their relationships with children.[6]

In Evelyn's case (see Chapter 2), her mother spoke to the nursery workers about her concerns regarding Evelyn's father. He used to take Evelyn into the bathroom and not let his wife, Evelyn's mother, come in. Evelyn's mother told staff that Evelyn had a red, sore bottom on occasion. She was clearly worried about her daughter but did not know how to voice her fears more directly. Perhaps she did not consider sexual abuse as a possibility. She needed someone to take her worries seriously and ask questions regarding the behaviours that made her worried.

In Jasmine's case (see Chapter 2), both her mother and her maternal aunt noticed that Jasmine's father was excessive in his creaming of her genitals when she was a baby. However, they did not talk about this with each other until Jasmine's behaviour became more distressed when she was older (about two-and-a-half years), and she began to disclose. Both of them had discounted their observations and not challenged Jasmine's father about his behaviour at the time.

Vanessa's mother was extremely anxious that Vanessa was being sexually abused by her father. She expressly asked Vanessa's father not to change the baby's nappy when he was left for short periods of time in sole charge. Despite her requests, he continued to change the child's nappy.

There were other indicators in all of these cases that were highly suggestive of sexual abuse. But in each case, while the primary caregivers were concerned about how the child was being handled, they were unable to follow up their concerns effectively.

This effective following-up of concerns is especially important if you are in contact with a known sex offender – known either because

---

6   See, for example, *Sounding the Alarm: Protecting children and young people from staff who abuse*, a training film (video) and resource pack. Details available at www.barnardos.org.uk/ resources/research_and_publications/books_and_tools_ tools_for_professionals.

he has a previous conviction or because you know personally that he has offended before. In these cases, it is important that you give your children explicit messages regarding this person and do not leave your children with him unsupervised. Many adult survivors of sexual abuse incorrectly assume that there is no risk to their children from their childhood perpetrator. But sexual offenders are unlikely to grow out of sexual offending behaviour.

Knowing who to discuss these concerns with and having them taken seriously is a first step in effective protection and reduction of possible risk. You may want to discuss your concerns with other adults in your network, or with professionals who also know your child, such as your GP, health visitor, your child's minder, nursery worker or teacher. It is crucial that this person listens carefully to what you have to say and helps you to think of ways to monitor the situation until the issues become clearer.

There are times when you may not be taken seriously. For example, when Vanessa's mother spoke to her GP about her concerns, he referred her for psychotherapy because of her obsession with the possibility that her daughter was being sexually abused. He did not consider that her concerns might be founded, did not implement any child protection procedures, and did not suggest that a formal investigation might be appropriate. However, when Jasmine's mother expressed her concerns to her GP, the doctor organised further follow-up, including a medical examination. The findings of this examination confirmed Jasmine's mother's worst fears, but she was offered ongoing support for herself throughout and after the subsequent formal child protection investigation.

If, as a primary caregiver, you are dissatisfied with the response you receive when talking to professionals about your concerns, you should not hesitate to get a second opinion. You can use a telephone helpline or voluntary agency to help you find someone who will take your concerns seriously. It may also be a good idea to take someone else with you when reporting your concerns. It can be helpful to have a clear description about any incident that is worrying, to be able to give details about what made this incident such a cause for concern, and to outline what you did. It is important that your concerns are recorded, either by yourself or by the professional you have contacted.

If the child's behaviour becomes less worrying over time, it is likely that whatever was distressing the child has now stopped. However, if sexual abuse was taking place, it is likely the child will continue to show signs of distress and cause you concern. If distressing behaviour continues, you may want to obtain more specialist advice from child mental health workers; your GP can refer you. You may also want to use independent organisations like MOSAC for support.[7]

If you find a plausible explanation for the child's behaviour, and you then try to rectify the situation, there should be some improvement in the child's behaviour if the explanation is correct. If there is no improvement, you may need to be more direct and ask the child what is bothering them.

> **Don't make the mistake that my mum and teacher did. They should have asked me. Nobody said to me – they just come down to the decision that it was 'cause of my sister . . . Know your child . . . when something does go wrong, you will know what you're looking for . . .**
> *Alison*

If the child can't or won't answer a general question, you may want to ask them about several specific possibilities, including unwanted touching. In all cases, trust your instincts and your knowledge of the child.

What to do if a child discloses sexual abuse to you

Before the situation arises, it is crucial that primary caregivers think

---

7   MOSAC provides support for non-abusing parents and carers of sexually abused children. See www.mosac.org.uk.

about the possibility that a child may tell them about an incident of sexual abuse. The essential elements to convey to the child when an unambiguous disclosure of sexual abuse has been made are very straightforward. You want the child to know that:

- they were right to tell
- you believe them
- you are going to help them get it sorted out
- the abuser was wrong to do that
- it was not their fault
- you are sorry it has happened to them (National Film Board of Canada, 1996).

If a child begins by asking you to keep something secret, it is important not to promise to do so. You need to know what they are going to say before you can decide what you need to do. You may say you wouldn't want to make a promise you might not be able to keep. If the child does not say anything more because you won't keep it secret, you should encourage them to tell someone else and perhaps suggest a telephone helpline such as ChildLine,[8] where they can talk confidentially. You also need to be clear that you would really like them to feel able to talk with you and to trust your judgement about what would need to happen next if you felt you could not keep their secret.

Your immediate reaction to what the child says is important.

> When I told her, she sort of like looked at me, you know, nothing . . . she just didn't want to know any more – like she just sat there, and I didn't know what to do – I'm just sitting on the opposite side and we started crying, and then she phoned the police . . . but she didn't talk to me. I was just sitting there on my own 'til they come . . .
> *Alison*

---

8   Tel. 0800 1111 www.childline.org.uk.

If the child tells you that someone you are close to is the perpetrator, it can be very shocking, even unbelievable. Remember the courage it has taken for the child to tell you. If you let your feelings show too much, it can be very inhibiting for the child or young person. They need you to be strong for them, to offer them comfort and support. Sometimes this is not possible immediately, because your grief or anger or shock is too great. In these cases, you will need to talk to the child later when you feel more in control. It is important for you to be clear that you are not angry with the child. Having your own source of support is essential, and you should find an adult you trust to talk to as soon as possible so you can support your child in the way that is most helpful to them.

It may be tempting to get a verbatim record of what the child is saying by audio- or video-taping the discussion. This should be avoided for a number of reasons. Most importantly, it would clearly interfere with the spontaneity of the child's telling. Caregivers do not generally record what children say to them. Organising a specific session so the child can say it all on tape will go against the child in a formal investigation, precisely because the primary caregiver will have had to set up the situation to record. It would also be unethical to record without the child knowing. It is much better to listen to the child, and ask a minimum of questions – just enough to be sure of what the child is saying and to help decide what needs to be done.

Do not probe unnecessarily or feel that the child needs to tell everything. It takes time for children to tell. They often begin with the least awful aspect and wait to see what the response is before revealing more details. So there is usually more to come.

However, if a child does start to give a lot of detail, it is not appropriate to stop them. You could take notes, telling the child that what they are saying is important. In this way, you can reassure the child that they are being taken seriously. The child's own words should be used – they should not be translated into adult language. If the child uses an idiosyncratic description, it can be helpful to ask them what they mean. Any non-verbal behaviour that goes with the telling should be noted, but no attempt should be made to interpret it. It is necessary only to get as much information as will be needed to know what to do next. Then the child should be told what will happen next.

If the disclosure is made to someone who has formal procedures to follow, for example, a teacher, these should be outlined to the child or young person as well as to the primary caregiver. There is no mandatory reporting of child protection concerns in the UK but professionals involved with children or with adults where a child protection issue becomes apparent are strongly encouraged to report their concerns to child protection agencies for further investigation. Only in exceptional circumstances, where the child's safety is at risk, should a formal investigation begin without the involvement and consent of the primary caregiver.

Ideally, a non-abusing parent will co-operate and help with a formal investigation. This includes giving permission for any necessary medical examination and investigative interview. Children need to know that it is alright for them to talk to professionals involved in the investigation and the child's caregiver should be sure to tell them this.

Protecting the child immediately after a disclosure

Your child's safety should come first. If someone within the family has been named as the perpetrator, the issue of removal may be raised by the professionals involved. Ideally, the alleged perpetrator should move elsewhere. This does not suggest guilt but indicates that adults who care for the child recognise that it is less stressful for the adult to move out for the time being than it is for the child. If this is not possible, it is worth thinking of a member of the extended family whom the child could stay with while the investigation is being conducted, or until the child's long-term protection is secured.

The child should not be badgered about what they have said already, or be put under any pressure to discuss it in more detail. Additionally, they should only have supervised contact with the alleged perpetrator, if any at all. This is because many children are put under enormous pressure to retract or take back what they have said following a disclosure of sexual abuse which names someone. Sexual offenders use very subtle (and sometimes not so subtle) tactics to intimidate both adults and children alike.

Consequently, there should be no telephone calls, as they are difficult to monitor; letters should be screened, with the awareness that they can be used to play on the child's loyalty and may contain coded messages; gifts are totally inappropriate and should not be allowed; actual contact should be supervised by someone who believes that the child may have been sexually abused and who could intervene if they felt the contact was not appropriate. In an age of text messaging and mobile phones, it has become increasingly difficult to control this aspect of a young person's life.

Inappropriate contact involves secrets being whispered, taking the child out of the room unsupervised (even to the toilet), and some forms of physical contact, such as sitting on the lap. If your partner is the subject of an allegation of sexual abuse, he will need to think carefully about how to interact physically with your child in a way that conveys affection for them but does not bring you added concern.

When Vanessa's mother asked her partner not to change Vanessa's nappies, he should have followed her request as this would have shown his respect for her and that he would put Vanessa's protection first. This pattern of stubbornly continuing to do something that the child's mother has expressly asked not to be done is often a characteristic of sexual offenders. It is not a lack of control they are exercising but the opposite – a wilful defiance of parental authority and an attempt to continue to exert control over the child and over you.

If the named perpetrator lives in your family and does move out while the situation is being investigated, your other children will need to be told in an age-appropriate fashion why he is staying somewhere else for a while (see Chapter 4). They may be very shocked and react strongly by blaming their sibling for causing this disturbance. Almost always they will take their lead from the parent left in charge. It is important to remember that other children in the family may also have been sexually abused but decided not to tell. This can explain some of the very strong reactions siblings sometimes have. You should not make assumptions that only boys, or girls, or teenagers, or stepchildren will be targets in any one family. Once someone has violated one child, they may violate others until they get the help they need to stop behaving in this way.

If the child protection services are involved they may ask for other children in the family to be interviewed or medically examined. This will be done to assess protection issues for all children in the family as well as offering other siblings a private forum where they, too, may disclose. Additionally, other children in the family may have information which supports or refutes what has already been alleged.

It is helpful if you can prepare the children for any medicals or interviews that may take place, and indicate clearly that it is alright to speak about family matters to the investigators. Without this permission, children may be very confused by the process and unlikely to be able to say anything.

It is important to recognise that, if a child is formally interviewed and then returned home to face their alleged perpetrator and continue to live with them while the investigation is going on, it is most unlikely they will repeat the disclosure which prompted the investigation, even if there is other evidence of sexual abuse, such as medical findings. They are very likely, in these circumstances, to retract or take back what they said.

Below is a list of reasons, generated in a girls' group, about why children do not tell:

1.   Feel they won't be believed.
2.   Too scared.
3.   Think it's their fault.
4.   Think they'll get beaten up.
5.   No one to tell.
6.   No one to trust.
7.   Don't know what will happen if they tell.
8.   Scared Mum and Dad will turn against them.
9.   Don't want the police involved.
10.   Brothers and sisters might be put into care as well as them.
11.   Think they are dirty.
12.   Worried about what friends will say.
13.   Don't want a medical examination.
14.   Too young to know what's going on.
15.   Wouldn't make a difference if they did tell.
16.   Already tried to tell and nothing happened, so gave up.

Children who have been sexually abused will almost certainly have been instructed not to tell. Often it is their mothers in particular who are singled out for exclusion by the perpetrator. Threats will have been made about what will happen if they do tell. This can include not being believed, being put in care, hurting their mother and, in some circumstances, explicit threats of physical violence to the child and/or to people – or even pets[9] – whom they love.

> **Why I didn't want to tell:**
> 1.   **George said he would kill me and I would be put in care.**
> 2.   **I was scared, mostly for my brother and sister.**
> 3.   **I felt too dirty and ashamed to tell my mum.**
> 4.   **I wouldn't have known how to tell her anyway because how do you tell your mum that her stupid boyfriend is messing around with her**

---

9   There is a strong correlation between animal and child cruelty (Hackett and Uprichard, 2007).

child's body when if anything it should be hers
he's touching not mine.

5.   At the time, I was scared of being put into care
so I thought it would be easier to run away.

Karen

It is necessary to remember that the threatening side of the person accused of sexual abuse will not necessarily be apparent to outsiders. Often, as long as the accused is in charge of things, their behaviour is charming. However, when discovered and confronted or challenged by others, they can become very bullying and abusive. In these circumstances, and also considering the fear, confusion and distress that may follow a disclosure of abuse for all concerned, it is hardly surprising that children often don't want to repeat allegations, and sometimes try to withdraw them.

If a child chose to tell you, they did so for a reason. This may be because they think you will take them seriously, believe what they say, and help them sort out the situation. If you are not the child's parent, you will need to make a decision about the best way to let the child's parents know what the child has said to you, and what you feel you should do with that information.

If you have any reason to believe that telling the child's parents might put the child at risk, you should contact a child protection agency first, or an outside support service such as a church, a community group or adult friends who may be able to offer a safe place for the child while the issues are sorted out or looked into in greater detail.

It can be tempting to immediately confront the alleged perpetrator regarding the child's allegations. But remember, only a tiny minority of perpetrators admit that the child is telling the truth. Some sexual offenders will admit initially, promise never to do it again, and give many seemingly plausible reasons for why it happened in the first place; and then when they are no longer under scrutiny carry on with the sexual abuse.

This is not a problem that will go away. If you try to keep the issue of sexual abuse within the family and not involve outside sources of support for yourself, you are likely to be swayed by the entreaties of the other adult over time, and may end up convincing yourself that it did not happen, or that it has now stopped. Try to get some thinking space for both the child and yourself. The alleged perpetrator should be asked to spend some time away from the rest of the family while decisions regarding the next step are made. The most important thing is to demonstrate that you and other protecting adults, who could be friends or relatives, are now in charge of the family.

If a child tells you about their experience of sexual abuse, they believe you will help them. They are also signalling to you that they want the sexual abuse to stop, and they need your help to stop it. Telling will be the first step for the child in moving from victim to survivor; believing and continuing to protect the child is your first step towards providing the best possible start for their recovery process.

References

Hackett S and Uprichard E (2007) *Animal Abuse and Child Maltreatment*, London: NSPCC

National Film Board of Canada (1986) *Feeling Yes, Feeling No* programme

Saradjian J (1996) *Women who Sexually Abuse Children: From research to clinical practice*, Chichester: Wiley

4

Establishing a context for recovery

If you are a non-abusing parent you are likely to be in shock if you hear of your child's disclosure or of a child protection agency's concern about your child. Help and support will be needed for you to come to terms with the possibility of sexual abuse of your child by someone you know, trust and possibly love. This is likely to be true for kinship carers and to a much lesser extent for foster carers. Having your worst suspicions confirmed can be unnerving and disturbing. Some foster carers also experience shock when they are confronted with sexual disclosures or explicit sexual acting out by their foster child, which can also negatively affect your view of the child you are caring for.

> **Please someone listen to me, tell me why it happened? Why did I not see it happen? Why am I the only person going through this hell? That's what I used to think when I lost my children to child sexual abuse. (Barnardo's, 1993)[1]**

---

1   Mothers of Sexually Abused Infants and Children is still going strong as a Barnardo's Project NE Division – see www.barnardos.org.uk/mosaic.

Discovering that your child may have been sexually abused by a member of your family is like being confronted with an unexpected bereavement. The unexpected nature of the information makes it harder to deal with. Even if you had an inkling that something was wrong, it is very shocking to discover that sexual abuse is at the bottom of that confusion. You will also be giving up a view you had about the person who abused your child – a view that was unlikely to include this possibility.

When someone dies, there are social and cultural rituals that help the mourning process. However, because of the stigma attached to sexual abuse, families touched by it find it difficult to share with others. There are no rituals to help lessen the distress, and the sense of shame and isolation is often overwhelming, even to those parents who believe and protect their child immediately. Many foster carers feel unable to discuss the details of their foster child's experience with people in their normal support network.

It takes a lot of courage to believe an allegation against someone you have known, possibly loved and trusted with your children.

> **It doesn't feel real. Every day is exactly like the next and on the outside nothing looks different. It wasn't until he admitted it – until then it was just a horrible nightmare. I kept thinking, 'There's no way it could be him. Somewhere there's got to be a guy in a dirty raincoat, because I've known this man all my life.'**
> **(*Liz*, quoted in Messud, 1991)**

This chapter helps you establish and maintain a context for recovery from an experience of sexual abuse. Recovery is not just something your child needs to experience. Everyone in the family will be affected by the disclosure of sexual abuse and will need help to come to terms with it. This chapter looks at what your child needs from you, what you need for yourself, and what can get in the way of you being an effective protector.

What the child needs

Your belief

Your child needs you to believe in and support them. Despite your
shock and confusion, you must put their need for safety and
reassurance first. A protecting parent should be able to demonstrate
unequivocally that they can protect their child and reduce the risk of
any further sexual abuse. As a foster carer it may be easier to offer
this unconditional belief to the child, although there may be certain
personal or family circumstances that make it specifically harder for
kinship carers.

We saw in the last chapter that if the alleged perpetrator is living
with the family it can be extremely difficult to guarantee protection
and reduce risk. If the perpetrator remains living in the family,
continues to deny that sexual abuse took place, and consequently
does not receive help for his problem, then the risk of future abuse
is extremely high, even if a believing non-abusing parent also lives
with the family. In part, this is because the perpetrator will have
undermined your child's confidence that you will be able to protect
them.

If the child protection services are involved and no protectors can be
identified within the child's immediate family, removal of the child
from the family home may be considered. The consequences of this
for the child, who may then believe that they are being punished,
can be devastating. So it is important to think about how you will
protect your child now and in the future.

In a situation with a named abuser, you need to:

- create a distance between the child and that abuser;
- surround the child with a supportive network of believing adults;
- give yourself time and space to let the fact of the abuse sink in;
- arrange support for yourself.

Mothers, as non-abusing parents, often carry the burden of guilt in sexual abuse. They are often also confronted with the starkest choices – their child or their partner. Many children in the care system struggle to understand their mother's choice to remain in often violent abusive relationships. This is often what they bring into therapy.

Society validates women who have relationships with men and actively encourages families to include both a male and a female parent. It is not surprising, then, that when women are confronted with that stark choice, they often opt for their partner. The economic dependence of mothers on fathers can be a very significant factor in deciding to disbelieve a child's allegations against their father. If you have never lived alone or been a single parent, it can seem an overwhelming prospect to contemplate. As a foster carer, you may need to think of the reasons why a woman would be unable to support her children. It is important that children, during their life cycle, develop a compassionate understanding of their abusive parents. This will help them to form better relationships themselves and work toward being protecting non-abusive parents.

It may seem easier to live with a "child who lies" than to confront the issue of a partner who sexually offends against your children; or to accept the minimisations and rationalisations of the offender and believe it won't happen again; or to hope that now it is out in the open, it will stop. There are generations of families who have pretended the issue of sexual abuse will just go away – and who have learned, to their cost, that it often doesn't. We have had referrals where brothers and sisters are involved in sexually abusing each other, repeating the experiences of their parents who were also abused by brothers, sisters, fathers or uncles, and where the mother is unable to stop this from happening. Often the parents are victims of domestic violence and were previous child victims of abuse.

If you are in the situation of hearing that your child may have been abused, and really can't believe it, use the list of indicators described in Chapter 2 to help you think about your child and the probability of sexual abuse.

> **If it comes to light and you can't believe it, just sit down and try to analyse things you may have been unsure about but didn't bother to question . . .**
> *Kiera*

If your child has a number of indicators, then you should start asking questions, not of the possible perpetrator but of your child. Sometimes, hearing your child's account will help convince you that the sexual abuse must have happened. The child's use of language and the description of familiar places or events will contribute to your belief in what they have said. This may be especially important if your child has told someone else but not yet been able to tell you directly. If this is the case, you need to let your child know that you have been told what they have said, that you are glad they have told, and that you believe them. Disbelief by a primary caregiver is devastating for the child and seriously impedes the child's recovery.

Your understanding

To begin the recovery process, it is important that you are emotionally sensitive towards your child. This can be difficult, because you will not only be in shock but also may be mourning the loss of a partner or experiencing a separation with an uncertain future.

Emotional sensitivity can also be difficult to achieve if your child's reaction to the sexual abuse does not conform to expectations. Many people expect children to show distress and rejection of the perpetrator. However, it is important to recognise that some sex offenders lavish attention, physical affection and possibly gifts on the child. They may also have given the child some positive parenting experiences as well as sexually abusing them. This makes it confusing both for the child and for the non-abusing parent.

If more than one child in your family has been sexually abused, they might react in totally different ways. One may be very quiet and withdrawn, whilst the other may be very angry and may act out. Sometimes only one discloses and others remain steadfastly silent or deny it. A protecting adult must be prepared for a wide range of often conflicting emotions that may fluctuate over time. In a foster family where siblings are placed together, this can be difficult to manage. Be aware that family patterns are hard to change and that sometimes secrets from the child's family of origin are kept alive by the siblings as a form of loyalty to their old family. This can include continuing inappropriate sexual activity.

If you have experienced sexual abuse in your childhood, you may find it difficult to disentangle your feelings from those of your child. This new episode of sexual abuse may rekindle feelings you thought you had dealt with. It is important to get help for yourself and not burden the child with your feelings. However, your messages that recovery is possible can be very powerful for a child to hear.

It can be especially devastating if your childhood perpetrator is also the person sexually abusing your child. You can feel you are to blame for your child's sexual abuse because you didn't tell when you were being abused. It is important to remember that you are not responsible for the perpetrator's actions.

If you find yourself overwhelmed with feelings that are getting in the way of understanding your child, it is essential that you find some support for yourself. You are your child's best support, and the best way to give your child support may well be to find help for yourself.

Being clear about who is responsible

It is important that a protecting parent conveys to the child that it is the perpetrating adult who is responsible for the sexual abuse. Regardless of the child's behaviour, it is an adult's responsibility *not* to sexually abuse. With young children this is easier, but with older girls, adults – including non-abusing parents – can become more confused, mistakenly apportioning blame between the child and the perpetrator. This is often due to the fact that many people view sexualised behaviour as triggering the sexual abuse rather than understanding that such behaviour in children is in fact a consequence of being sexually abused (see Chapter 5).

Non-abusing parents might also apportion some blame to themselves: 'If only I had done this or noticed that...' But with hindsight we are all better protectors. Sexual abuse is maintained by secrecy and plays on people's naivety and on the ambiguity of physical contact and public closeness between the perpetrator and the target child. This is especially true for female perpetrators who can more easily access children and be involved in intimate caring for them without raising alarm.

There are many and complex reasons why sexual abuse is not detected or suspicions not acted on. If it happens, it is not your fault or the child's, and there is nothing to be gained by blaming yourself. You may want to talk with other adults about why you think you are partly to blame, but your child needs you to be clear that the abuser is responsible for what he did. Given the high rates of drug and alcohol addictions, it can be all too easy to blame the perpetrator's behaviour on drugs or alcohol. But this is just a smoke screen, as the thought to sexually abuse will have been present already and the drugs or alcohol only served to overcome internal inhibitors.

What you need

Many of the things your child needs, you will need as well. You may need some distance from the perpetrator, especially if he is your partner. You will need friends and relatives to believe and support you through this experience, and not just in the short term. The pain and upset may feel keenest immediately after the shock has worn off, but often you can still be struggling with the issues and the consequences for you and your children years later.

Give yourself time and space

Having the time and space to work through the feelings brought up by a disclosure of sexual abuse is absolutely vital. For mothers there will be a mixture of conflicting feelings, especially if the perpetrator was also a partner. The feelings regarding your lover or partner need to be dealt with separately from those you have as a parent.

Don't be too quick to decide that everything has been sorted out. Remember, children often disclose in stages, so there may be more to come. Sometimes, other children in the family cannot disclose until the abuser has moved out. Whilst a perpetrator's denial may make it hard to believe your child, sometimes an admission lulls a protecting parent into thinking that everything will now be alright. Having time with your child, but without the abuser, is crucial for both of you. You need to be able to respond to your child and think about what you want to do.

Sex offenders will bring pressure to bear on both the child and their protector to keep quiet about the sexual abuse. So once you have managed to physically distance yourself and your child from the perpetrator, it is essential that you talk to someone about what has happened. Keeping the abuse secret only protects the abuser. He needs to know that you will not hesitate to go outside the immediate family for help and advice and that he needs to do some work on his problem before he can return, if this is something you are considering. If you feel certain your child has been sexually abused, then before considering any return home you should ensure that you and your child feel safe and ready to resume the relationship, and that he admits to the abuse and is prepared to get professional help for his problem. This can be difficult in contact situations where children can be pressurised to retract their allegations.

Even with professional help, it can be several years before everyone is ready to try to live together again. You may decide during that time that you don't want to live together any more. It is realistic to think in terms of 18 months to two years before things seem normal again. So be generous with your time for yourself. Don't let anyone rush you into making a decision about the family's future until you are ready. Be sure to talk with other supportive and trusted adults before you make any decisions. You should also be confident that your child is beginning to recover from the experience of sexual abuse and that you have helped them in that process. This will offer greater protection in the future, as living with a known sex offender requires the highest levels of monitoring and vigilance on the part of the protecting parent.

Getting support for yourself

There are lots of issues you will need to explore, and this should not be something you do on your own. Other members of the extended family will be confronted with similar feelings of shock and possible disbelief. But their knowledge of everyone involved, coupled with their slight distance from the situation, may make it easier for them to be helpful. Their support is essential to break down the isolation and devastation so many mothers feel following the discovery of sexual abuse.

Although the immediate impulse is to keep it quiet, finding people you can trust to talk to about the abuse is just as important for you as it is for the child. You will need someone who believes and will not judge you, but who will also be honest about the risks involved; someone who will help in practical ways, such as taking the children off your hands for a while, or giving you the space to moan or complain about the situation.

Discovering sexual abuse within your family means you have to be a parent first, putting to one side your healthy adult need for love and affection. Many mothers find that by concentrating on being strong for their children and being a parent first, they manage to cope with the situation better in the short term (Hooper, 1992).

> **If you feel you are not getting the support or help you need, just believe in your own feelings and fight for your child alone, no matter what.**
> *Kiera*

It is important that the support you seek is selective. In a crisis you can be very vulnerable and needy. In such a state, you may talk to everyone about what is happening (although keeping quiet about it is more usual). However, talking indiscriminately could jeopardise confidentiality about your child in the wider community. Many people still do not understand sexual abuse, and will make unkind and insensitive remarks both to children who have been sexually abused and to parents. Many non-abusing parents turn to professionals for help and support. This may involve your child's teacher, your GP or health visitor, or the child protection agencies. Statutory agencies should be a resource and support for non-abusing parents. There are also specific voluntary agencies and resources for non-abusing parents.[2]

In many areas, there are groups for parents whose children have been sexually abused. These can be a very useful source of support as the other parents will be going through, or may have gone through, the same things as you are.

> **The group has helped me face really hard times by letting me know that I am not the only mother going through hell because my children were abused.**
> **(Barnardo's, 1993)**

The increased monitoring a vulnerable child needs when sexual abuse has taken place is best carried out by someone who knows the child well, who cares for and loves the child, and whom the

---

2   For example, MOSAC, which provides support for non-abusing parents and carers of sexually abused children. See www.mosac.org.uk.

child can trust. These protectors usually come from within the child's nuclear and extended family. Social workers, by virtue of the demands on their professional time, can offer only a minimum level of protection. Teachers have to spread their professional attention across a number of children. This is why it is important for you to be able to talk about the sexual abuse with your family, friends and wider network as well as with professionals.

Talking about it with family

It is important that the other children in the family are given some information about what has happened, especially if it results in the removal of either the child who has disclosed or the perpetrator. This is also true for children in foster families. Siblings need to know, in age-appropriate language, what has been disclosed. For young children this can be minimal but still needs to clearly convey important information.

Children may ask questions that do not have immediate answers, such as 'When will he be back?' It is important that you are honest with them. It is better to say you do not know than to make up something. Younger siblings may well want to know at a later stage why their father/sibling no longer lives with them or sees them any more. In a fostering situation, you will need to be more general in the explanations you give your own children.

If a parent who is the subject of an allegation moves out while the allegation is being investigated, it may be more helpful to be vague about the concerns until the investigation has been completed. If children indicate they know something more specific, it signals to the protecting parent that a more detailed response is required. Many looked after children don't understand why criminal cases don't proceed following their disclosures. They can be confused if some children remain living at home or if new children come along but are not removed. These are difficult issues to address.

Children's requests for information about experiences of sexual abuse often occur at different developmental stages. This is equally true of requests for information from non-abused siblings. They may, when they are much older, ask for more specific information that may have led to a dramatic change in their family's life.

Child sexual abuse encourages both adults and children to keep secrets. It is not easy to start talking openly and honestly about something that has been kept a secret for so long. The feelings of guilt on the part of both parent and child can be very strong, and can make it extremely difficult to explore some issues in depth.

> [My sister] has been asking like, who her . . . who her dad is . . . And, me and my mum, we just both look at one another and sort of, like, think. My mum said that my sister's just gonna think he's dead. If she wanna know, somehow she'll find out. I'm just wondering how she's gonna react when she finds out . . . If she finds out . . . she'll wonder why we didn't tell her . . .
> *Alison*

It can be useful to have someone outside the family to help you talk about the sexual abuse with your children.

> It needs to be highlighted that parents need help on how to speak to the child after abuse. My knowledge of this was very little . . . Once there's more help for the parent, then of course it must help the child and be less stressful.
> *Kiera*

Sometimes being with other mothers who have been through the same experience is a first step to being able to talk about it at all. Foster carers often support each other or receive support, training and advice from the agencies working with looked after children.

Do you feel you are the only parent going through hell?

> Do you think you have been branded as a bad person
> walking about with a label pinned on you saying your
> children were sexually abused? . . . Don't try to take all
> the blame for what happened . . . It is a great help to
> know you are not the only one, as I thought.
> (Barnardo's, 1993)

When involving members of your extended family, it is important to
pick someone you trust and on whom you can rely. Kiera's (see
above) sister and mother were especially supportive and were able
to help her deal with her partner's sexual offending.

Involving friends and community

Just as you need to choose whom to talk to in your extended family,
you need to be selective with regard to your friends and those in
the wider community. You may also need to help your child with
this by identifying whom outside the immediate family they can talk
to about the sexual abuse. Whomever you choose needs to believe
it has happened and be discreet, as it is important to protect your
child from ignorant comments and prurient interest. Your child
needs to know who knows what about them and their experience
of sexual abuse.

Many women and children from minority ethnic communities feel
they will not be supported by their community if they disclose sexual
abuse from within the community (Wilson, 1993).[3] They often feel a
conflict of loyalties because most external child protection agencies
do not represent the interests of their communities and have a
history of intervening inappropriately (Mars, 1989).[4] So it is
extremely important within minority ethnic communities that child
protection as an issue is taken seriously by the community. This will

---

3   See also www.southallblacksisters.org.uk, which has campaigned since 1979 on issues
     of violence against women, or Da Silva S (1992) *Sexual Abuse and Asian Women*
     (unpublished MA thesis), Lancaster: Lancaster University. There is still very little published
     about sexual abuse within BME communities.

4   See also Khadj R (1991) *Black Girls Speak Out*, London: The Children's Society.

convey to the child and any protecting parent that support and resources are available from within the community.

Statutory child protection agencies operate in the dominant language – English. In a multilingual family, the potential protector may not speak the dominant language. Access to English may be controlled by the perpetrator, thus restricting the options of both the target and the possible protector. In such instances, it is essential that the non-abusing parent get help from someone within their community.[5]

It is easier for all communities to think of sexual abuse as something perpetrated by an outsider. Yet it is all too clear that sexual offences against children are most likely to be perpetrated by someone known to the child. This is true for all communities. However, for minority ethnic communities, child protection also involves protecting children from racist attacks, which are clearly perpetrated by individuals who are not members of the minority ethnic community. But it is important that protecting the community from outsiders does not lead to a denial that anything negative, including sexual abuse by members of the community, can happen within the community. A denial that it happens silences the survivors within any community and often presents them with what should be an unnecessary choice – belonging in silence, or speaking out and finding there is no place within the community for their reality. This would have a very negative impact on the child's recovery process and the community would then become a refuge for those who inflict damage on its own members. By tackling issues of child protection, communities make themselves strong enough to both confront sex offenders and facilitate the recovery of those who have been sexually abused.

Blocks to being an effective protector

There are some factors that can get in the way of being an effective

---

5   NSPCC has a phone line specifically for the Asian community.

protector. Some of these are discussed in this section.

Not believing

Not believing your child is the biggest block to being an effective protector. If you are finding it really hard to believe what your child has said or what others are telling you has happened, it can be helpful to talk about this with someone else. Try and sort out which bits you are struggling with.

You may need to think about what would help you believe or be convinced it has happened. Remember, admissions by abusers are rare. There is often no medical evidence, no police charges and no conviction. Listen to what your child has said to you or to other people. Sometimes foster carers are waiting for their foster child to talk about sexual abuse with them. But this can be difficult for the child, so it is helpful to let them know what you know about them. The training course, *Parenting a Child who has been Sexually Abused* (Hellett and Simmonds, 2003) is aimed at helping you to do this.[6]

If you believe your child has been sexually abused but not by the person they have named, tell them you believe they have been sexually abused and you want to make sure it does not happen again. Many children continue to make allegations because the most important one has not been handled appropriately. They can develop reputations as liars. It can be really difficult to disentangle the truth within many stories, parts of which may be true and parts false.

If you continue to disbelieve your child, you will be hurting them and it is likely that the abuser will continue with the abuse. Having the child labelled as a liar is a perfect cover for someone to continue to sexually offend. The child can also think that you know it is

---

6   See resources developed by BAAF to support foster carers in their task:
     www.baaf.org.uk/res/pubs/books/tprograms.shtml.

happening even though you *say* you don't believe them. Perfectly adequate protection plans can be devised without knowing who has sexually abused the child. Sometimes we can become too focused on knowing the identity and forget the more important task of keeping children safe from further abuse.

Vulnerabilities

Sex offenders often target women or children who have vulnerabilities, such as a physical or intellectual disability. This is precisely because they can increase the woman or child's dependency on them. It can be more difficult to be an effective protector for such vulnerable people because it may be harder to access outside sources of support. In some cases, the perpetrator may accentuate the disability and increase the dependency purposefully.

Disabilities that may increase a person's vulnerabilities, and impact negatively on their capacity to protect themselves and their children, include communication difficulties such as deafness, where oral communication may be limited or the person uses sign language, and physical disabilities that restrict the mobility of a child or a possible protector. The freedom of movement a potential protector would need could be severely curtailed and controlled by someone who wished to increase the physical dependency that is already present.

To reduce these vulnerabilities, potential protectors must have access to an outside source of support that would be able to help if sexual abuse was an issue. There are support groups to which disabled women can go, but unless the group has already considered the issue of child sexual abuse, then the response may not be appropriate or helpful. Group members may be too shocked to help; they may disbelieve the woman or blame her for what has happened; they may ostracise her, thereby increasing her isolation and possible dependency on the perpetrator; they may feel too uncomfortable even to discuss the issue. Some members of the group may not have children, and so thinking about protection and parenting might not be something they have begun to address.

It is important for all protecting adults, including those with disabilities, to identify and establish a network of potential support for themselves by raising sexual abuse as an issue in their current group. It is becoming increasingly clear that sex offenders not only target women whom they perceive as being vulnerable, but also will target children with disabilities who may be less able to protect themselves from sexual abuse. Any vulnerable member of the community can be targeted for a whole range of abuses, including sexual abuse.

Vulnerabilities such as a physical or intellectual disability are not necessarily a block to effective protection, but it is useful to develop protective strategies for yourself and your child.

Survivors and parenting

Many people believe that having a history of sexual abuse yourself will impact negatively on your capacity to protect. In the majority of cases, this is unlikely to be true, as often those people who have experienced victimisation or discrimination are the quickest to recognise abusive situations.

If you have been sexually abused as a child, you may be more sensitive to the signs or indicators that your child is being sexually abused. You may be more able to believe a child's disclosure, and convey that belief to the child unequivocally. But if you have been sexually abused and never disclosed this information or talked about it to anyone, discovering that your child has also been subjected to this experience can be very disturbing to you personally because it may activate traumatic memories that you had managed to put out of your mind.

Working on your own experiences of sexual abuse after discovering that your child, too, has been a victim is possibly not a good idea. Recovery work in sexual abuse often makes you feel helpless and like a child. This feeling would be incompatible with what your child needs from you at this point – a parent who believes and who can help them to recover. The last thing a child needs is to sense that you are feeling especially vulnerable. Children who have been sexually abused are often very sensitive to adults' needs, and if they sense that their experience disturbs you they may choose not to talk to you about it.

So, if you decide that this new disclosure has brought up unresolved feelings for you about your childhood experience, it may be helpful for you to find someone to help you talk through your feelings. It is important for your child's recovery, however, that you remain a parent to them; that you are clear it is not their fault that you are remembering things you would rather not; and that you are not angry with them for disclosing the current abuse.

Ongoing abuse

If a potential protector is still being sexually abused by her childhood perpetrator, or is currently being physically and/or sexually abused by her partner, it will be extremely difficult for her to be an effective protector for her children. She should take immediate steps to protect herself from the abuse, and check that the child is not at risk from the violence she is experiencing (Nicarthy, 1991).[7]

Violence, which can seem so personal, is likely to be more generalised, and the violent man may well be attacking more than one individual. Women leaving violent and abusive partners may think their children are better off remaining, and that the violence and abuse will now stop. This is unlikely to be true.

---

7   There is now a wide range of publications available about domestic violence – see www.womensaid.org.uk.

Domestic violence between parents seriously compromises the protective capacities of both parents. Children can be frightened to let possible protectors know about sexual abuse for fear of the repercussions, both for themselves and for possible protectors. If children witness their father beating their mother, and they themselves are subjected to his physical, as well as sexual, violence, it is most unlikely that they will perceive their mother as someone who could protect them. They are more likely to perceive her as a victim like themselves. Establishing parental authority in situations like this can be very difficult and demoralising for the non-abusing parent.

Violence encourages children to be passive and submit, or to become violent themselves. Rather than learning to protect themselves and others from physical and sexual violence, children who witness violence in their immediate surroundings are likely, at best, to learn to live with it; at worst, they are learning to do it themselves.

Clearly, it is not possible to begin recovery work in such a hostile environment. The safety of both the child and the possible protector must be secured first.

Maintaining the context for recovery

It is important to keep protection to the forefront in your family and your community. This will help to reduce the risk of re-victimisation and will encourage everyone to take personal safety seriously. As your child grows up, it is appropriate for them to take on some responsibility for their own safety. Teaching them to be assertive, to be clear about what they like and don't like, to talk to someone if they are confused, to let you know where they are going, with whom and for how long, are all part of developing self-protection skills. If other adults in your network are also giving these messages to children, the positive impact will be that much greater. For those children who have already been sexually abused, their recovery work will be facilitated by a more receptive community that can deal with unresolved issues as they arise. So it is vital to establish a wider context for recovery within which any child and any possible protector can begin to recover from an experience of sexual abuse.

A readiness to believe that child sexual abuse happens prior to a specific incident occurring makes it more likely that the potential protector and their children can remain connected to their community. In communities where sexual abuse is considered impossible, a disclosure which challenges that belief often produces ostracism, not for the perpetrator of the sexual abuse, who frequently claims privileged status by virtue of gender or class, but for the child who discloses, and sometimes the parent who tries to protect. Raising the issue of child sexual abuse before it happens will empower future protectors and encourage children to tell if they are being sexually abused.

To be an effective protector, it is essential that you have access to other adults who support and affirm your authority within the family. It is also important that there is a place for you to express your feelings of guilt, shame, anger, sadness and betrayal, which at the same time recognises the continuing parental tasks you still have to provide. You will probably need a separate forum to deal with any personal feelings that are making it more difficult to help your children to recover from the experience of sexual abuse.

Establishing a context for recovery is not the sole responsibility of a non-abusing parent. It needs to be much wider – a responsibility embraced by the whole adult community. This will not only help protect all the children of the community, but also make it easier for those who do experience sexual abuse to tell, and to begin their recovery process. A believing, supportive response from a protecting parent is clearly that much more potent if the same protective and corrective messages are echoed by the wider community: You are not alone. It is not your fault. It should not have happened. We are sorry that it did happen. You were right to tell, and together we are going to get over it.

References

Barnardo's (1993) *Mothers of Sexually Abused Infants and Children leaflet*, London: Barnardo's

Hellett J and Simmonds J (2003) *Parenting a Child who has been Sexually Abused*, London: BAAF

Hooper C (1992) *Mothers Surviving Sexual Abuse*, London: Routledge

Mars M (1989) 'Child sexual abuse and race issues', in Robson J and Giltinan D with Kenward H (eds) *After Abuse: Planning and caring for a child who has been sexually abused*, London: BAAF

Messud C (1991) 'Mother courage', *The Guardian*, 21 April

Nicarthy G (edited and adapted by Jane Hutt) (1991) *Getting Free: A handbook for women in abusive situations*, London: Journeyman

Wilson M (1993) *Crossing the Boundary*, London: Virago

protection agencies become more active in uncovering sexual abuse for a younger generation of survivors. The connection between an early episode of sexual abuse and later sexual exploitation is clear.

However, because not enough research has been done with people who were sexually abused in childhood but do not use the mental health system as adults, it is easy to assume that all victims of sexual abuse will experience devastating psychological consequences. This is probably not the case for most survivors; some people are able to recover from their experiences of childhood sexual abuse without professional help or intervention. This should encourage non-abusing adults to adopt a more proactive, protective stance. It is very likely that the silent survivors who have made positive recoveries from the early childhood trauma of sexual abuse have met with sympathetic and helpful responses from those around them.

In the short term, immediately following disclosure of sexual abuse, the child often experiences increased feelings of fear, depression, anger, hostility and aggression (Finkelhor and Browne, 1985). Since many sex offenders use a combination of threats and bribes to secure a child's silence and compliance, the child will probably be frightened and anxious after disclosing. This is why the child's safety and keeping a distance between the child and the perpetrator are emphasised in Chapter 4, which discusses establishing and maintaining a context for recovery. Knowing the specific threats the perpetrator used is important, because protectors can then reassure the child that these threats will not materialise.

> . . . he used to say I'd be taken into care if I ever told.
> My mum would just put me away . . . or they'd take me
> away from my mum.
> *Alison*

Unfortunately, long delays in child care proceedings are especially stressful for children. It means they have to wait to find out where they are going to live. If sexual abuse has been an issue, ongoing proceedings often make it harder for them to talk about and make sense of their experiences. The child will always have in the back of their mind the possibility of returning home. If they are also having ongoing contact, they can be put under enormous pressure to retract or may be silenced from disclosing further. The silencing tactics can be very subtle, and in small communities "contact"can be accidental, but still have an enormous impact on the child.

For example, one small boy had talked in his therapy sessions about his uncle doing something sexual to him and his little brother. The case was still in proceedings with the little boy and his brother living in a foster placement. While on holiday with his foster carers, he unexpectedly saw his uncle. In this case, the uncle approached the foster carers, asking for directions. Only later did the boy tell his foster carers that the man asking for directions was his uncle. Nothing was said to the little boy but the impact of this chance meeting was dramatic. He refused to talk about what had happened at home or to continue in his therapy.

If the abuse goes on, or if the child's concerns and emotional distress are not addressed, then the child's feelings of anger, hostility, depression and aggression will become exacerbated and potentially more disruptive.

> I get really angry towards myself because I think what happened was my fault and because I think I should have stopped it; also the fact that although I was drunk, I let so many things happen; also because of things that happened when I was sober but honestly I just did it to stop it going on and to keep him quiet, to stop giving me hassles.
> *Lisa*

The types of emotional difficulties that can follow from sexual abuse include: self-destructive behaviour; high levels of anxiety; isolation and stigmatisation; low self-esteem or self-esteem derived from sexual activities alone; difficulties in forming trusting and safe relationships; re-victimisation and further exploitation; drug and alcohol abuse; and sexual maladjustment (Finkelhor and Browne, 1985). The majority of abused children will have some difficulties in specific areas, and some exhibit all of these difficulties. In a small proportion of cases, the child will show no outward signs of distress and be able to get on with age-appropriate tasks.

Areas of concern

This section focuses on aspects of a child's development that may be distorted by an experience of sexual abuse. As a protecting adult, you need to be giving the child the knowledge and experience of interacting with a non-abusing adult. This should help to correct some of the distortions and facilitate the child's recovery process.

Developing an appropriate body image and healthy self-esteem

Most children develop a sense of personal space at a young age. This includes a basic understanding of "where my body begins and ends". For a child who is sexually abused from infancy, this fundamental concept of separateness and the establishment of an appropriate body image does not develop appropriately. The child can become intrusive and show no understanding of privacy or personal space. Their touching is often over-familiar and their need for close physical contact overwhelming. This physical contact is often highly sexualised, and adult recipients experience intense discomfort when approached. This can lead adults who come into contact with the child to be physically rejecting at a time when the child's need for physical reassurance is likely to be great.

The child may need to be taught how to give and receive non-sexual physical affection. This is especially important in a fostering context. We want children to benefit from an alternative family placement. They need to experience positive, affectionate and nurturing touch from both male and female parental figures. They will need to be reminded about personal space and praised when they begin to assert their own need for privacy and personal space as well as respecting that of others.

Not all children are sexualised by the experience of sexual abuse. More commonly, the child feels used and dirty. They can feel insignificant, especially if no one has noticed they were being sexually abused. Taking the time to ask and to be concerned directly challenges the child's belief that they are of no worth or value. They may neglect themselves and not attend to their most basic physical needs; or they may become disconnected from the messages their body is giving them, such as 'I am hungry' or 'I am no longer hungry'. This is more likely to be the case where there has been pervasive neglect as well as inappropriate sexual touching. The invisibility they feel may be matched by their appearance, as is the case with severe anorexics, or may be totally at odds with their physical size or presence. One young woman who shouted all the time when she spoke said she had to speak loud or she would not be heard. So the distortion of body image and body messages can be extremely profound and sometimes not based on reality. Only constant feedback from protecting adults can begin to change this perception: 'I can see you. I can hear you. I do believe you exist.'

Many children who have been sexually abused feel as if they have been profoundly and irreversibly damaged by the experience. Suzanne Sgroi refers to this as the "damaged goods syndrome" (1982; see also Gil, 2006). Alternatively, some children will come to perceive their self-worth only in terms of their usefulness as a sex object. This can lead to the child relating to the world through sexual activity of one kind or another, sometimes almost exclusively. Some children will need help to control the strong sexual feelings that have been triggered by the inappropriate sexual contact. They have developmentally inappropriate sexual knowledge that cannot be taken from them. It may be important to correct sexual misinformation they may have acquired, as well as providing an appropriate context for them to explore their bodies safely.

The child may be used to an audience and be very insistent on involving others (both adults and children) in sexual interactions. Protecting adults need to give the child alternative ways of interacting. For example, if a child tries to give an adult an open-mouthed kiss, a protecting adult can say, 'No, children and adults don't kiss that way. This is how they give each other kisses', and then follow up with a clear, unambiguous kiss on the cheek.

Protecting adults need to ensure that any sexual behaviour the child is manifesting is contained in a private place, such as the child's bedroom. It may also be necessary to ensure they are not hurting themselves when they are being sexual. Many children who have been sexually abused and who are showing very sexualised behaviour can be hurting themselves when they masturbate, either through their own rough handling or by inserting objects into their genitals and bottoms.

The sexualisation described above is not an amplification of normal childhood sensuality. The child's sexual feelings are likely to be overwhelming and grossly distorted. The child will lack the cognitive skills to understand what is happening to their bodies and over time may become addicted to the heightened physiological state the sexual abuse produces – in some cases a potent combination of both fear and sexual arousal.

Developing a positive self-image

In considering the impact of sexual abuse on the development of a positive self-image, it is important to consider the wider social influences on this process for all children. There are very powerful messages about gender and ethnicity that impact on the formation of a positive self-image. Not all of these messages are positive, but clearly, significant adults in a child's life can counteract to some extent those messages that encourage a child to feel negative about aspects of themselves.

It is important to consider how sexual abuse will impact on a child's understanding of self. For boys who have been sexually abused by men, the issue of becoming a man can be problematic. Unless a boy who has been sexually abused by a man has access to other non-abusing males, he may assume that all males become perpetrators as they become men. If he does not want to follow this perceived pattern, his identification as a male is in jeopardy. Some gender stereotyping is also internalised by girls, who may believe all males will be abusive. Within a fostering context, these scripts around gender can be corrected through role modelling and discussions that challenge such stereotypes. Safe caring policies that exclude male caregivers are depriving children and young people of an opportunity to experience a male caregiver differently.

A boy who has been sexually abused by a man may want to convince himself that he has not been damaged by what would be considered by many to be a homosexual encounter, and he might then become deliberately sexually aggressive towards or preoccupied with females. A boy who has been abused by a man will have to deal with wider society's homophobia, as the shared gender of child and perpetrator often becomes the focus rather than the adult sexual exploitation of the child. Fears about issues relating to homosexuality are thought to be one of the main reasons boys are reluctant to disclose sexual abuse by men, despite the fact that many male perpetrators who target boys also target girls and women, and would describe themselves as heterosexual.

For black children, dominant racist perspectives of black and minority ethnic sexuality will impact on the child's experience, especially if the sexual abuse is disclosed to someone from outside the community. The child might not want to disclose under these circumstances, or alternatively, these views may confirm the child's own limited experience of the community. Black men can be portrayed as sexually voracious; black girls as sexually precocious; black women as sexually promiscuous; Asian men as sexually repressed; Asian women as sexually exotic. There are numerous stereotypes combining sexuality, ethnicity and culture promoted by dominant groups. There will also be sexual stereotypes promoted within minority ethnic communities that the dominant group is not aware of. It may be difficult to talk about this, but at least acknowledging this aspect of identity is essential. Sometimes cross-cultural placement and therapy seems a safer place to begin, but the debate needs to be opened up sensitively within communities.

Sex offenders as a group will employ any stereotype that facilitates the sexual abuse and serves to rationalise their behaviour. The child is unlikely to know this and may believe the stereotypes to be truly representative of a particular gender or ethnic group. In this way their identity can be profoundly damaged, as they may try to reject aspects of themselves that they associate negatively with their experience of sexual abuse.

Learning to have and express feelings appropriately

Children who are sexually abused live in an internal world of secrecy and confusion. This can make it difficult for them to express a whole range of different emotions and feelings, and leads to a very restricted affective range. They are allowed, or allow themselves, to express only certain feelings. Much of the anger they feel when being sexually abused must be repressed (they are not aware of it) or suppressed (they are aware of it but are not free to express it directly). If the experience was also traumatic, this will also impact on the expression of feelings.

> Often I don't know how to express my feelings . . . and I become frustrated and depressed. I am also moody and very sarcastic on the subject of life. That is when I want to cut myself or run away because I don't know how to express myself.
> *Lisa*

Anxiety, fear and depression may be overwhelming but they are often disguised – either as unrelenting hyperactivity or under a flat, inexpressive exterior. Many adults diagnosed as suffering from post-traumatic stress disorder (PTSD) exhibit what is called a numbed responsiveness to the outside world. Sometimes this can be seen in children as well.

Keeping powerful feelings in check all of the time is extremely difficult. Sometimes there will be dramatic, explosive outbursts. This can include suicide attempts or violent attacks on others.

> **If I get in an argument with someone, I think back and I start building up a hate for that person, and like, bringing all the blame down on that person. Sometimes I get pretty violent because of it.**
> *Alison*

> **I would love to punch him until there was no more energy in me and he could feel the anger inside me. Sometimes I feel so angry I just want to hurt myself but I don't . . . and I'm confused and I just have so much tension inside of me and I pace round the room thinking of things that I could do to myself even though I don't really want to. I need to release the anger in me but I can't. I hate myself and feel ugly and dirty for doing what he wanted. I can't stand myself.**
> *Lisa*

Many children who have been sexually abused do not feel entitled to any feelings at all. Given that their feelings have been ignored by the perpetrator, and misinterpreted or not recognised by a possible protector or protectors, this is not surprising. Additionally, children and young people who have been sexually abused are likely to receive strong messages from others regarding what they should feel about their experience, rather than being allowed to discover their own feelings. Other people's feelings, and expectations about how the child should feel, can be pushed on to them. This can range from an expectation that they should be angry when they may not be, to pressure to get over it when they are not yet ready to do so.

It is important that the recovery process helps the child or young person learn to recognise and identify their feelings and then to express them appropriately. This can take a long time, and can involve a whole range of experiences, possibly including therapeutic work.

> [To begin with] everyone [in my group] was, like, isolated from everyone else. We were just sort of sat there, and none of us wanted to talk about it. Some of the girls were pretty angry – you couldn't get straight talk out of them. They'd just say, like, they wanted to kill him . . . [The group] helped us get out some of the anger that we had bottled up inside. [In family sessions with Mum] it was good to be next to her to hear what she was feeling.
> *Alison*

Sexual abuse severely restricts the range of emotions and feelings that can be expressed, not only by the child but also by others in the immediate family.

Support and a safe context to explore feelings are an essential part of the recovery process for everyone involved. Support for the child and caregiver is essential.

> I have my own feelings on the abuse and haven't made her feel the same as myself . . . I have tried not to let her see how I feel about the abuse and how I hate her daddy for doing it. I don't want her to have to choose sides . . . I want her to be central right now and maybe when she's older, she will feel different or understand the reasons for my feelings.
> *Kiera, Jasmine's mother*

Judging safe people and situations

Children who have been sexually abused by a parent figure have been betrayed. It can be difficult for the child to decide how to judge future relationships when such a primary one has been violated. Children either learn to rely on their personal experience to judge individuals or remain confused and essentially vulnerable to inappropriate relationships because of their inability to judge what or who is safe.

It can be helpful to give children and young people a problem-solving approach to assessing people and situations rather than a list of safe places or people. Such an approach encourages children to learn how to judge situations and people, and suggests that they let others know where they are, what they are doing and who with.[2]

It can also be helpful to identify situations that may be risky, especially for adolescents, who quite appropriately should be taking some responsibility for their own personal safety. This can include using drugs or drink where their ability to protect themselves would be negligible; going unaccompanied or with people they don't know to a place they don't know; or getting into a car with a driver who is clearly drunk. It may also be important for protecting adults to teach children the assertiveness skills they will need to say no and get away from situations that don't feel comfortable.

Developing an appropriate sense of responsibility

Many children who have been sexually abused feel responsible.

> I feel guilty for hating him because I sometimes feel
> sorry for him thinking that what happened was my
> fault and because of me he is locked up.
> *Lisa*

---

2   The three stranger questions – Do I have a Yes or a No feeling about doing x? Does someone I trust know where I am? Can I get help if I need it? – are from National Film Board of Canada, 1986. If the answer is no to any of the questions, the child shouldn't go without reference to a trusted adult.

I used to think it was all my fault . . . it took a very lot
of encouraging . . . that it wasn't my fault, it was theirs
. . . I always thought I made them do it.
Natasha

Q: Who do you think is responsible?
Alison: *I've learned this [laughing] – him. I still feel like I
should have told sooner – and told him 'No'.*

*Q: And if you had told him 'No', what do you think he
would have done?*
Alison: *Just done it anyway [laughs].*

*Q: Because, let's think – you were giving out 'No'
signals . . .*
Alison: *I just used to sort of cringe. I can just remember
when he took me out once – he was buying stuff and I was
standing there, and I was going, 'I don't want it.' I thought if
I didn't take nothing off of him, that I wouldn't have to do
anything. I can remember saying, 'No, I don't want that –
no.'*

Q: Who do you think your mum thinks is responsible?
Alison: *Him – because he's an adult – he should have had
more sense.*

Q: Do you believe that?
Alison: *Sometimes . . .*

*Q: What do you think it would take for you to stop
feeling responsible?*
Alison: *I don't think I ever will.*

Sex offenders encourage the child to feel responsible because this
encourages the child's sense of entrapment, which facilitates the
continuation of the abuse. The child's sense of responsibility can
often become distorted. They can feel overly responsible even for

things that are clearly not their responsibility, as in Lisa's case where she felt responsible for her perpetrator being jailed. Frequently, children feel guilty and think they need to be punished as well. They can inflict the punishment on themselves by self-harming or trying to kill themselves.

If it is the child who is removed from the family home and not the perpetrator, this further complicates the issues of who is responsible and who is to blame. Failure to believe a child's disclosure, whether on the part of the non-abusing parent or professional child protection agencies, will almost certainly make the child think they are in the wrong, it is their fault and no one believes them. By implication, it suggests to the child that sexual abuse did not really happen, that they should not have told about it, and if removal occurs, it is because they were wrong to speak out and are being sent away or punished for doing so. Children can also continue to try to protect both the perpetrator and the non-abusing parent by remaining quiet, retracting their allegation, or attempting to make things better by taking over caring for the family. Sometimes the contact arrangements for children who are looked after are not safe enough, so they are exposed to abusive situations and the possibility of re-abuse whenever they have contact. This is very damaging and confusing for the child.

In addition to feeling responsible themselves, many children also locate some of the responsibility with their mothers or the non-abusing parent. Helping a child or young person to understand who is responsible for the sexual abuse is one of the first steps towards helping them to recover. This means being clear that the abuser is responsible for his actions; not the child or the non-abusing adult. As the child matures, they will have to learn to take responsibility for their own behaviour too, and to know that a history of childhood sexual abuse will not excuse them from taking personal responsibility for their actions as they grow older. Protecting adults need to help clarify who is responsible for what, and help the child develop a realistic sense of personal responsibility.

Developing an understanding about right and wrong

The sexual abuse of children is fundamentally tied up with the issues of right and wrong, which form the cornerstone of moral development. Unfortunately, society is equivocal about how wrong sexual abuse is. This is conveyed in a number of ways, not least of which are the mitigating circumstances that can be taken into consideration when sentencing a convicted sex offender (Mitra, 1987; Yates, 1990; Kelly et al, 2005). Mitigating factors include a plea of guilty, the father had a genuine affection for his daughter, and/or she has had previous sexual experience. Older girls in particular are often seen as partially responsible for their own sexual abuse. In 1993, there was an outcry when a judge, sentencing a convicted sex offender, described the eight-year-old victim as 'no angel'.[3] This kind of statement implies the child has some responsibility for the sexual abuse. Legally, this is construed as contributory negligence. This concept is frequently used in rape and domestic violence cases where the actions of the women are seen as contributing to the commission of the crime.

In the absence of a clear statement that sexual abuse is wrong, and the belief in such a statement by everyone a child comes into contact with, that is, society at large, it may be difficult for children who have been sexually abused to develop the necessary repugnance to sexual abuse that would prevent a victim becoming a perpetrator. Many children and young people become stuck wanting revenge on their childhood perpetrators and in a twisted way exact their revenge by hurting others.

Juvenile sex offending is extremely serious, and more recent research has indicated that brothers and stepbrothers formed the largest group of named perpetrators within the family, and outside of the family the largest single category was boyfriend/girlfriend (Cawson

---

3   Judge Ian Stanforth made this statement in 1993. In October 1993, he conditionally discharged two men convicted of unlawful sexual intercourse with a 13-year-old girl, saying that she had tried to satisfy her sexual desires (*The Guardian*, 29 July 1994). In the same issue, Judge John Whitely is reported as fining a 44-year-old man £50 for sexually assaulting a six-year-old girl. These are old examples, but still shocking in terms of reflecting attitudes which I am not sure have changed very much.

et al, 2000, p 80). However, juvenile sex offending is often minimised, not only by the juveniles, usually male, involved, but also by their parents and sometimes by child protection agencies as well. The consequences for the child who is targeted or victimised are often just as devastating as if the offender were an adult. The consequences will be worse if the activities are not identified as sexual abuse and no protective measures are taken. It is unfortunate that the impact of juvenile sex offending and younger children's sexual bullying is minimised, as there is good reason to believe that, dealt with effectively at a young age, the likelihood of further sex offending can be significantly reduced (Ryan and Lane, 1994).[4]

Protecting adults must convey unambiguous messages about the rights and wrongs of sexual abuse, making it clear that the *action* itself is wrong, not the getting caught. Protective adults need to let children know that sexual abuse is wrong; that, while there may be explanations for the abuse, there are no excuses; and that protecting adults have a responsibility to prevent it from happening. These statements can be made regardless of the outcome of a case of sexual abuse. In Alison's case, for example, the perpetrator was acquitted on a legal technicality. This did not change Alison's mother's mind about what happened, nor any of the workers involved in supporting Alison. The damaging consequences of the acquittal were reduced by the clear position maintained by the protecting adults.

Developing positive relationships

Sexual abuse affects a child's capacity to make and sustain relationships. Closeness and intimacy may seem threatening. Adults as protectors may seem an alien concept.

---

4   More recently, see the sophisticated analysis provided by Dr Eileen Vizard and her team in relation to this client group, Vizard E, *et al* (2006).

Many young people who have been sexually abused do not know how to negotiate relationships, especially non-sexual ones. They may exchange one abusive relationship for another. They can also be very dependent, almost unable to function on their own. This is due to the low self-esteem, guilt and confusion they can feel about the sexual abuse. The secrecy surrounding the sexual abuse may also have made it difficult to think of establishing independent relationships outside the family. Alternatively, the child may be pushed prematurely into other intimate relationships.

> It affected me in going out with boys, 'cause, like, everyone was going out with boys and I was thinking 'I AM NOT going out with a boy'. It took me until I was, like, nine or 10 to really go out with a boy properly. And I thought, 'Alright, this is alright. Now what's the next step?'
> *Natasha*

When Natasha came to speak to me when she was leaving care at 18, she was in a relationship with a man almost three times her age. He accompanied her to the interview. She was very open about why having a relationship with an older man worked for her. Reflecting on this over the life cycle would be interesting. This reminds us that the effects of sexual abuse can be different at different stages in our lives. Sometimes significant life cycle changes like leaving home, getting involved intimately or becoming a parent activate feelings from past experiences. It can help to talk about them. The same is true for parents or foster carers who themselves may have been sexually abused. Parenting a child with similar experiences can stir up a lot of confusing feelings and may lead to a re-examination of previous thoughts and feelings regarding the abuse. This is not necessarily negative. It can be helpful to say to a child, 'When I was your age I felt that way but now that I am older [or a parent], I see things differently'.

A child may be distrustful of adults and may be overly reliant on peer relationships. This may be quite functional, as good friends can help the recovery process begin. However, if the young person's relationships are sexualised, then there is an increased risk that they may be exploited sexually once again. A high degree of dependency makes them very vulnerable and easily targeted by sex offenders, who will exploit the young person's healthy need for a relationship. Pimps will use this tactic to break in young girls and boys into prostitution. They often "rescue" the child from an abusive situation. They spend time listening, taking care of the child and offering gifts, ranging from a place to stay, to food, money, drugs or drink – all of which increase the child's dependency on them. They then exploit this dependency by asking, often forcing, the child to repay the kindness.

A child may decide to avoid all relationships as being too risky. They may try to take care of all of their own needs and will make only superficial relationships with people, avoiding any intimacy.

Protecting adults need to prepare themselves for the distrust and rejection they will experience when trying to renegotiate or begin a relationship with a child who has been sexually abused. Appropriate adult–child relationships will have been eclipsed by the inappropriate relationship between a sex offender and his target.

It is also important to encourage appropriate peer relationships, especially same-sex friends. There is enormous pressure on young people to be involved in romantic relationships without recognising all the complexities and complications that may exist, especially for someone who has a history of childhood sexual abuse.

Talking about an experience of sexual abuse within the context of a safe, trusting relationship that does not involve sexual intimacy, such as with a parent, friend or professional helper, is the most important part of the recovery process. This will enable the child to develop their sense of self-worth as a person and give them the best possible basis from which to develop intimate relationships. Friends and choice of partner are probably the most significant factors in securing a healthy adjustment to adverse childhood experiences.

Developing a positive sexual identity

Sexual abuse can distort an individual's sexual development. The child may have been given misinformation about sex by the perpetrator, or may have made incorrect inferences themselves as a consequence of early developmentally inappropriate sexual contact. They may be unclear about reproduction, or believe their internal organs were damaged by the experience. Often these misperceptions may not be evident until adolescence, when it is developmentally appropriate for a younger person to want to establish more intimate relationships.

The child or young person will need information on sex, biology and reproduction. It will be difficult for them to make best use of the sex education offered in school because it will be hard for them to judge what is developmentally appropriate knowledge. To ask questions might indicate to peers that something has happened. So it can be helpful to provide some idea about what other children of a similar age might know.

Many young people who have been sexually abused find it difficult to share their history of sexual abuse with prospective sexual partners. They worry that it will be used against them, or that it will turn their partners from them. Sometimes they feel they do not know their partners well enough to share this part of their life. But consensual sexual activity can unintentionally trigger memories of the original sexual abuse, and this can lead to a variety of consequences such as distress during sex, avoidance of sexual intimacy or withdrawing from sexual activity during sex. This is further compounded by then having to deal with the partner's disappointment, upset and/or confusion over what has happened.

Having a flashback to a sexually abusive experience whilst having sex with a partner is extremely unpleasant. If it is not shared, then the consensual sexual intimacy can become perverted, possibly by making a consensual experience a re-creation of the original sexual abuse. It can also reactivate the issue of secrecy. Hopefully, a sensitive partner will pick up the non-verbal signs that indicate something is wrong, and will feel confident and concerned enough to ask why. With young people, this requires a high level of maturity.

Children who have experienced sexual abuse can be sexually stimulated and become accustomed to the feeling of being sexually aroused most of the time. In a sexually abusive household this can be functional. However, when they are no longer being sexually abused, children can still be left with strong feelings of arousal and not know what to do, other than make inappropriate sexual overtures to others or masturbate.

Many young women who have been sexually abused continue to have sexual relationships with men, sometimes compulsively. This is often not perceived as being problematic, because it represents a socially accepted expression of sexuality. But the compulsive quality is indicative of the distress and confusion the young woman bears, and is likely to increase her vulnerability to a whole host of risks. It is also likely to compromise her sexual health and reproductive capacity.

Teaching young people to be protectively discriminating about sexual partners is especially important if they have also experienced sexual abuse. They can mistakenly assume that high levels of sexual activity demonstrate that they have not been damaged sexually by the abusive experience. It is also likely that they will have learned to "turn themselves off" to avoid feeling or even thinking about their past experience, especially during sexual activity, which often triggers the unwanted memories or sensations.

Homosexuality is often seen as a negative outcome of sexual abuse, and equated with damaged sexuality. But compulsive and indiscriminate heterosexuality may be a consequence for girl children sexually abused by men, and, in this case, homosexuality for the young woman might be a more positive way for her to continue exploring her sexuality with fewer triggers to traumatic material.

For boy children sexually abused by men, there can be a fear that having had this experience means they are homosexual. In this case, it is important to stress the importance of choice in sexual orientation.

Being sexually abused by someone of the same sex does not make someone homosexual. Being sexually aroused by someone of the same sex in the context of being sexually abused does not mean the experience was really wanted or that secretly the victim is homosexual. These issues need to be raised sensitively when helping children and young people who have been sexually abused by someone of the same sex.

It is also necessary to recognise that, in the wider social context, heterosexuality is encouraged. This wide social acceptance of heterosexuality often leads to heterosexual sexual abuse, which involves either adult male sexual abuse of girls or adult female sexual abuse of boys, not being taken seriously. In contrast, homosexual sexual abuse which involves adult male sexual abuse of boys is frequently seen as being more perverted than heterosexual sexual abuse. Adult female sexual abuse of girls is often not even considered. These attitudes reflect wider societal views regarding sexuality and sexual orientation; it may be necessary to challenge these views in order to help a child recover from *any* sexually abusive experience. What is most important is for the child or young person to feel positive about the sexual choices they have made, and comfortable with their own identity as a sexual being.

It is also important to consider that for some children or young people it may not be possible to reclaim their sexual identity, as it is so powerfully connected to their experience of sexual abuse. Their feelings about their sexuality and their desire to share this aspect of themselves with someone else may change over time. A period of celibacy may be extremely helpful and a lifetime of celibacy may well be a constructive resolution.

High levels of sexual activity, coupled with an early childhood experience of sexual abuse, increases the risk of several health problems, including cervical cancer, infertility and sexually transmitted diseases including HIV and AIDS. Protecting adults will need to raise these issues explicitly and almost certainly well in advance of when they would be raised with a child who had not been sexually abused. Young people are unlikely to raise these issues with you – or with their sexual partner – and will need a protecting adult to take the lead, either through discussion or providing written materials that might help.

Developing good communication skills

Living with sexual abuse creates an atmosphere of secrecy in the family. Communications cannot be trusted, as the child can never be sure what they mean. The child who is being sexually abused may be hyper-vigilant – waiting and watching for the signs that might indicate that another episode of sexual abuse is about to happen. This, in part, explains why so many children who have been sexually abused have difficulty sleeping. They try to stay awake, as if being awake will stop the sexual abuse from happening. At least having some notice of an impending bad experience reduces its traumatic impact.

The child, as he or she becomes older, will appreciate the duplicitous nature of the sex offender – often someone admired by others. Sex offenders can speak eloquently against sexual offending and yet continue to sexually abuse. They can convey contradictory messages simultaneously. The consequence for the recipient of such contradictory messages is confusion.

Sexual abuse can be framed as loving. The child can be told they liked it or they wanted it, when their own experience is the contrary. A child can be made to give contradictory messages, such as saying they liked it when they did not. If their bodies responded to physical stimulation, they can feel confused because one part of them may have said "no" but another part of them said "yes". They will need help to sort out this confusion.

The child may need you to be clear that you hear them and that you are trying to understand what they are going through. You may need to teach them to listen to you and to ask you questions if they don't understand. You may need to do the same to them. You need to give them feedback about what they are communicating to you.

When helping a child to recover from sexual abuse, adults may be confronted by contradictory messages that make it difficult to know how to respond to the child. The child can describe something that is very distressing and show no signs of distress. They may laugh when other people would cry. It is important to remember that the child, in order to survive the experience of sexual abuse, will have learned to smother their feelings. They may also need help to learn how to express their feelings, both verbally and non-verbally. Tell them you don't know how to respond to them when they give you contradictory messages. This may also be a signal to you that the child or young person has been traumatised by their experiences and is still in a post-traumatic state activated by triggers that remind them of their trauma.

If the child has become very sexualised by the experience of sexual abuse, they may continue to use sexual gestures and postures to ask for comfort. They often do not realise there are other ways of doing this. They may also be unaware that most people would consider their manner sexually provocative. Until they are given feedback about how they behave, and shown alternative ways of behaving, they will continue to use the same behaviours and methods of communicating that they have always used. It is difficult for protecting adults to tackle this, but essential that they do so.

Developing appropriate personal authority issues

Sexual abuse is not only a sexual violation of the child, it is also an abuse of the authority adults have over children.

> He knew that he had power over me to do it. I couldn't
> do nothing back.
> *Alison*

The experience of sexual abuse impacts on the child's understanding
and experience of authority. Unfortunately, the abuse of authority is
endemic in our society. Teaching children that it is wrong to bully or
force someone to do something they do not want to do is fraught
with problems because that is so often how people do things and
get what they want. The serious impact that bullying can have on a
child or young person's life is widely recognised, with some reported
cases of suicide indicating that bullying was the trigger to such
drastic action.

The experience of sexual abuse can reinforce a child's perception
that the world is composed of abusers and the abused. It can lead
them to avoid authority, view it suspiciously and expect it to be
tyrannical. They may not recognise the responsible exercise of
authority. So it is particularly important that the parental authority of
the non-abusing parent is reinforced after the discovery of sexual
abuse (Smith, 1994).

It is also important that the child who has been victimised sexually
feels comfortable with their own authority so that they can be
responsible for their behaviour. They may need help to learn the
difference between assertiveness and aggression. Having lived for
years with a bully, it is unlikely that they will not have learned a lot
about bullying.

Children who have been sexually abused are very perceptive in
relation to power hierarchies. They understand and will challenge
authority, or ally themselves to those they perceive as powerful. This
can be functional as it is a useful skill to have in a society that is so
preoccupied with authority. But it can also be dangerous. The
abused child can be labelled manipulative, which carries very
negative connotations. And there are clear gender differences, with
males being encouraged to assert their superior position in the

power hierarchy and females being punished for assertive or aggressive behaviour.

The issue of authority is relevant to all of us, but for those who have been sexually abused it is especially so. All too often children do not see authority being used effectively, even by those adults who seek to protect them. Also, the sex offender will have undermined anyone else's authority as a way of reducing its potential protectiveness.

Protecting adults are in the unenviable position of trying to establish the responsible exercise of authority while at the same time benefiting from the privileges bestowed on adults. But by struggling with these issues and discussing them with the children and young people you come into contact with, you will begin to challenge the authority of the abuser, which for so long remained unchallenged in the child's life.

Dealing with the consequences

This chapter has outlined some of the consequences of sexual abuse and drawn your attention to areas of concern for many children and young people who have been sexually abused. It is important not to underestimate the role your support and belief play in a child's recovery. However, the protecting parent does not have the sole responsibility for dealing with all the consequences of sexual abuse.

Recovery work is very demanding and often emotionally draining. The pain, distress, sadness and anger experienced by protectors can go on and on, and they are likely to feel lonely, isolated, frightened and overwhelmed by the task of helping their child recover.

> **I hope and pray we never go through anything like it again. We are still trying to get our lives back to normal . . . I don't think Alison and myself will ever get back to the way we were . . .**
> *Moira, Alison's mother*

You may need to remind yourself how things really were. Now that the sexual abuse has been discovered, it is possible to recover – or even discover – parts of yourself, your relationship with your child, your friends and your community. Do not be afraid to ask for help and support for yourself and your child. You may think you are managing or you may feel utterly overwhelmed.

> I know that as an ideal to be strong for your children is crucial and right and necessary; but from my experience of not just myself but of other mothers in my situation – we have been broken wrecks for all kinds of reasons . . . Being strong has been something we tried to do and usually failed miserably, taking our children down with us.
>
> Sometimes it is possible to feel that "professionals" can expect the impossible because, in most cases, they do not know what it actually feels like and cannot comprehend the devastation . . . Most of us can be left feeling guilty that we are never strong enough, loving enough, tough enough, un-neurotic enough, good enough . . .
> *Tilla*

But remember – it would be unusual if you didn't feel like that. Protecting adults frequently have to take all of the responsibility and yet rarely have the authority to get what they need for themselves or their children. It is likely, in the circumstances, that you have done more than you think.

> I used to think my mother was to blame. I don't now. At the group, we talked about it and I think she did enough for me. She believed me. All the other girls there, their mums didn't believe them and they were all in foster care.
> *Alison*

Being at home with her mother who believed her made it possible for Alison to manage her recovery work, take responsibility for herself and her future, and want more out of life than childhood memories of sexual abuse. A supportive and believing foster placement can make all the difference for a looked after child. Foster carers who can talk about what has happened, and think with the child about the impact of those events on the child's life, open up the possibility of different ways for the child to think about themselves, their future and the families they will make.

References

Cawson P, Wattam C, Brooker S and Kelly G (2000) *Child Maltreatment in the United Kingdom: A study of the prevalence of child abuse and neglect*, London: NSPCC

Finkelhor D and Browne A (1985) 'The traumatic impact of child sexual abuse: a conceptualisation', *American Journal of Orthopsychiatry*, 55:4, pp. 530–41

Gil E (2006) *Helping Abused and Traumatized Children*, New York, NY: Guilford Publications

Kelly L, Lovett J and Regan L (2005) *A Gap or a Chasm? Attrition in reported rape cases*, Home Office Research Study 293, London: Home Office

Mitra C (1987) 'Judicial discourse in father daughter incest appeal cases', *International Journal of Sociology of Law*, 15:2, pp. 121–48

National Film Board of Canada (1986) *Feeling Yes, Feeling No* programme

Ryan G and Lane S (eds) (1994) *Juvenile Sexual Offending: Causes, consequences and correction*, Lexington, MA: Lexington Books

Sgroi S (1982) *Handbook of Clinical Interventions in Child Sexual Abuse*, Lexington, MA: Lexington Books

Sharland E, Seal H, Croucher M, Aldgate J and Jones D (1996) *Professional Intervention in Child Sexual Abuse*, London: HMSO

Smith G (1994) 'Parent, partner and protector: conflicting role demands for mothers of sexually abused children', in Morrison T, Erooga M and Beckett R (eds) *Sexual Offending Against Children: Assessment and treatment of male abusers*, London: Routledge

Summit R (1983) 'The child sexual abuse accommodation syndrome', *Child Abuse & Neglect*, 7, pp. 177–93

Vizard E, McCrory E and Farmer E (2006) *Links between Juvenile Sexually Abusive Behaviour and Emerging Severe Personality Disorder Traits in Childhood*, London: National Child Assessment and Treatment Service (NCATS) Research Unit

Vizard E, Hickey N and McCrory E (2007) 'Developmental trajectories associated with juvenile sexually abusive behaviour and emerging severe personality disorder in childhood: the results of a three-year UK study', *British Journal of Psychiatry*, 190 (supplement), pp. 27–32

Yates C (1990) 'A family affair: sexual offences, sentencing and treatment', *Journal of Child Law*, April/July, pp. 70–76

6

The healing process

This chapter suggests some of the issues you might want to take up with the child to begin the healing process, to help you to identify when professional help might be needed and to provide information so that the child receives the best possible help. It also looks at different types of interventions that can help children heal and at ways of dealing with challenging behaviours.

But before any healing can begin, the child needs to be safe. First of all, you must have ensured that the sexual abuse has stopped and that the child is surrounded by a network of protecting adults.

It may be that you and other protecting adults can provide the best context for a child to recover. Children may prefer to talk to the people they are closest to, rather than to a professional who is also a stranger. (This is generally true for younger children, whereas adolescents often prefer to talk to someone outside the family.) Certainly, the more knowledge and information that protecting adults have about sexual abuse, the issues which may arise, and how best to help a child recover, the more likely a child's speedy and full recovery.

Professional help, such as therapy, can certainly help sexually abused children and support the protecting adults, but it would be far more beneficial for the child if *all* the surrounding adults had access to the skills and expertise of professional safeguarding workers and could employ these to support children in their day-to-day living. Professional help should ideally back this up, not replace it. So, the following section provides information about issues that are likely to arise once sexual abuse is disclosed, to give you the skills to best help your child begin to recover.

Beginning the healing process

The initial disclosure, of course, marks only the beginning of the healing process. There will probably be more to tell. The more the child is able to speak about their experience, the quicker they will be able to put it behind them. But in some cases, the child will not want to discuss the experience immediately. It can help to have a safe distance between an event such as sexual abuse and the talking part of the recovery process.

You may want to leave it to the child to indicate when they are ready to talk. But be careful that you are not encouraging the child to remain silent or colluding with the natural tendency to want to forget the experience and not talk about it any more. You should signal to the child that you know about the abuse and that you are available if they want to talk about it at some stage in the future.

In some cases, the child may choose to start talking about the abuse at an inconvenient time, when there are lots of people around, for example, so that the conversation will not be private. If this happens, you should acknowledge that they have indicated a desire to talk about their experience, and then make a time when it would be better to continue the discussion.

Children may want to talk about the abuse at times when they remember or have flashbacks to the experience.

> The memories I have always seemed so far away but now they keep getting closer and I remember things that happened many years ago. It's really scary. I can be doing something really normal and then suddenly I get the recalls of the past. Just little things but they really wind me up.
> *Lisa*

This can be in situations that remind the child of the original sexual abuse, such as bedtimes or bath times. In these situations, it is important that you reassure the child that they are now safe.

> Even now I think it still has an effect on me . . . I was really scared and I didn't want to go to my maths lesson . . . my teacher reminded me of my abusers – they were tall, he's tall and you have to look up like that . . . he's got a moustache . . . and, like, talks in a deepish voice. It scares me, but not enough for me to really show it.
> *Natasha*

You may want to change routines around any trigger activities so they are less likely to remind the child or young person of their sexual abuse. It can be helpful to change bedrooms or rearrange the furniture in an effort to reduce unwanted memories. Living in the house where it happened will be difficult for the whole family, but particularly for the child who has experienced the sexual abuse.

Children often do not like to talk face-to-face about their experience of sexual abuse, preferring to talk whilst doing something else, such as washing the dishes or being driven in the car when the adult is in the front seat and they are in the back seat. The more distant approach seems to help the child discuss some of the more worrying aspects of their experience.

As the experience of telephone helplines has taught us, children will talk about their experiences of abuse on the telephone, which allows them to be as anonymous as they wish and gives them maximum control. They don't have to be looked at and so feel less exposed, and they don't have to deal so much with the reactions of the person listening.

For protecting adults who are supporting a child in the healing process, it is important to get the right balance between being interested and available, and being too intrusive and curious.

> **[It's important] to let the person that it's happened to do some of the talking – like I noticed with my social worker when she was talking to me, she'd try and push words into my mouth, like, you know – and that's not what I wanted to say.**
> *Alison*

It is important to recognise that the recovery process is not accomplished overnight, but is ongoing. Every developmental phase may bring up new issues. Do not be surprised if the sexual abuse seems to become an issue at a later stage in the child's development. For example, many young women who were sexually abused become concerned about protection issues when they themselves become mothers. Adolescents can become confused, worried or distressed when they want to be physically intimate with peers but do not know how their earlier experience of sexual abuse will impact on this.

Remember that if such issues, concerns or problems do arise later, it does not mean that the work done earlier was not helpful. It merely indicates that more work should be done now, when new situations have triggered different concerns.

Occasionally, children will talk about the abuse too much. When they tell for the first time adults may – and should – stress that the child was right to tell, and encourage the child to feel good about having told. However, the danger of talking too much is that the child might then start telling everyone, which can put them at risk. Other children may tease them about it; adults and children who are not aware of how to deal with sexual abuse may disapprove of and/or blame the child; and any adults who have a sexual interest in children may hear about it and recognise that this child will be an easy target. It is important that children are given identified trusted adults to whom they can talk. In school, it can be helpful to have one identified teacher who is aware of the sexual abuse. In the extended family, particular relatives can be identified as sources of support for the child.

It is important that all those who care for the child recognise the child's right to privacy and guard against the indiscriminate disclosing of information regarding sexual abuse. The appropriate involvement of the wider network surrounding the child needs careful consideration. And the child will need to know who knows about their experience and who they can talk to if they want to. If you are in any doubt about who to involve in the child's wider network, seek advice.

Getting professional help

Recovery can take many forms, and if the child can put the experience to the back of their mind and get on with their childhood, this may be very functional. It does not mean they will never have to do some additional work on their experience of sexual abuse at a later stage, but additional work may not have to be provided by professionals. Often, life experiences in and of themselves can be healing. For example, a close friendship, a good relationship with a parent or parent figure, an understanding partner, can all contribute to a successful resolution of a sexually abusive experience.

> If it came back as a worry I'd share it with someone,
> 'cause here [at the foster family] I was always taught
> "You share your worries", like a problem shared is a
> problem halved. I was always taught that . . . like my
> next door neighbour – she even wrote me a song on

it . . . "Lean on me, when you're down and feeling blue,
you know you can lean on me".
Natasha

In general, if a child is able to get on with developmentally
appropriate tasks, there may not be a need for additional help,
beyond information for parent and child, possibly some counselling
and access to resources. But you should look for professional help if,
after the abuse:

- the child is finding it difficult to do things other children of the same
  age can do;
- the child is exhibiting problem behaviours which are beyond normal
  limits and have gone on a long time;
- commonsense approaches have been unsuccessful in trying to
  reduce or eliminate problem behaviours;
- the child is old enough to participate in treatment and, where
  appropriate, wants help to sort out the problems.

But remember, professional help should ideally *back up* support that
you, and other members of your child's network, will need to give
your child, not *replace* it. You will need to have the skills to deal
with, for example, difficult behaviours that may result from the
child's acknowledgement of the abuse and the work they do with
professionals. If the child goes into therapy, for instance, they are
likely to explore very traumatic issues that may trigger behavioural
problems. If the adults surrounding the child on a day-to-day basis
have no idea how to manage these behaviours, then the child's
recovery is likely to be hampered. The surrounding adults will need
the skills to reassure the child that these behaviours – which, as we
have seen, may previously have been functional to surviving the
sexual abuse – are no longer necessary, and to teach the child to
cope with their feelings in a different way.

If it is clear that a child or young person requires additional
professional input, it is important that the primary caregiver feels
confident in the skills, and is comfortable with the manner, of the

professional who is undertaking the treatment work.

You can sometimes refer your family or child directly to a professional, especially if you are paying for your sessions. There are also self-help networks that provide good support and advice. Referral for professional help is either through your GP, who should know what is available in your area, or through Children's Services, who may be able to offer some help themselves. Most agencies involved in recovery work would want to know that the safeguarding issues have been dealt with, as there is no point offering treatment to a child who is not safe.

Don't hesitate to ask questions about the service being offered. It may seem intimidating, but good professional workers should help to put you at your ease and explain clearly and simply what they do, why they do it and how they think they can help.

The following is a series of issues you could discuss prior to the child or young person starting treatment. They should form part of establishing the therapeutic contract between the worker, the primary caregiver and the child.

Expertise in and approach to sexual abuse work

Not all professionals will have had training in child sexual abuse as part of their qualification training. Do not assume that because someone has a professional qualification, they know about sexual abuse. Always check this, and if the professional does not have the relevant training and experience, seek other help. Additionally, the professional's views about sexual abuse might not correspond to your own. You may not feel comfortable with the way in which your child's experience is handled. If this is apparent at the outset, it may be better to seek help from someone whose views more closely approximate your own. It is important that the professional helper is clear that sexual abuse is a real experience that is often traumatising and always disturbing for the child, and that it is the adult perpetrator who is responsible for the sexual abuse. If the professional helper is at all disbelieving of the child's experiences, it is doubtful that they will be able to help the child recover.

It may also be important to know to what extent sexual abuse will be the focus of the therapeutic work. Some professional helpers will work specifically on issues related to the sexual abuse, while others may employ a broader life perspective or be very non-directive in their work. If a child is too young to decide what will be helpful for them, it is important for the primary caregiver to help decide what suits an individual child's needs. Some children respond well to a very focused approach, while others benefit from a more non-directive style. The key issue must be what is best for the child at a particular stage, and to what extent the sexual abuse will be recognised as shaping the child's current behaviour or emotional distress.

Use your knowledge of the child to help you choose the professional help that fits with your child's temperament. A brief, focused groupwork experience is often extremely helpful, as many children gain a lot from being with other children who share the same experience of sexual abuse.

Liking and feeling comfortable with the person who is going to work with your child is very important. Remember, you are entrusting your child's healing to this person, so you should have confidence in their ability to help sort things out, and they should be able to tell you how they think they can achieve this.

It is important that the child or young person knows that the professional is aware that sexual abuse has happened. Otherwise, a lot of valuable therapeutic time can be wasted, because the child keeps the sexual abuse secret, as they've previously been told to do, and the professional is overly sensitive and does not raise the issue until the child does.

Confidentiality

Issues around confidentiality need to be clear at the outset. The difference between secrets, confidentiality and privacy needs to be spelt out for the child or young person and the primary caregiver. Because sexual abuse is often surrounded by secrecy, this aspect of starting therapy can be very confusing for everyone. Therapy should be a special time for the child. It is private and what is shared between the child and their helper is confidential. However, if the child or young person wants to share the contents of their therapy sessions, they should be able to do so. It is important to ensure that therapy, while private, is not secret, as this is perhaps too similar to the secrecy promoted by the perpetrator when the child was being sexually abused. If the child is in a group, they will have to recognise the need to respect other group members' privacy.

Sometimes, confidentiality can be interpreted too rigidly, whereby primary caregivers are not given any information at all about the sessions. This is unhelpful because it appears to promote secrets between the child and one protecting adult which are not shared with another protecting adult. Clearly, this will be more of a problem with younger children than with adolescents, who are more likely to understand the difference between secrets and privacy.

However, it needs to be made clear from the beginning what information is private to the session and what will be shared with the adults who have a responsibility to protect the child or young person. Generally, anything that would indicate the child is going to harm themselves or cause harm to others should be shared outside the session. If the child makes new disclosures, this should also be shared outside the session. This does not include amplifications regarding the original allegation, although technically this could constitute new disclosures.

Feedback

This issue is related to confidentiality. Primary caregivers should have some feedback regarding the sessions. With older children, this can be done as a progress report that is discussed privately between them and the professional before it is given to the primary caregiver and/or the professional who referred the child for treatment. Children and young people can appreciate why adults need to have some idea about what is being discussed in their healing work.

It is also important to remember to give the child or young person feedback about their progress as well. Often the recovery process can seem very slow and changes hard to detect. Periodic reviews can be useful to remind everyone just how much has been covered already.

Availability between sessions

It is important to know how available the professional helper will be between sessions, especially if a crisis arises. This may be an issue for the primary caregiver and for the child, particularly for adolescents. Professionals should be able to give clear messages about their availability. Professional helpers are not the same as friends and consequently are not as available as a friend or parent might be. This artificial construction of the helping session is part of what makes it useful and enables the abused child or young person to talk about painful experiences. The sessions are limited, usually an hour in individual sessions or longer for group or family work. The meetings take place in a neutral venue and not where the child was sexually abused. The child or young person is not expected to deal with the helper's feelings or problems, as they would be with friends.

The helper is there to listen carefully and give their full attention to what is being discussed. To do that, appointments are made at regular intervals. They can be from several times a week to once a month. Usually, individual and group work is weekly. Family sessions may be fortnightly or monthly. With weekly sessions, the child has to learn to manage their feelings as best they can between sessions. Sometimes this is very hard, which is often why primary caregivers and the young person concerned want to know if they can telephone between sessions if they get scared or upset. Sometimes it can be helpful for the child to write between sessions, because on the day of the appointment the child may not remember what it was that seemed so unmanageable before.

Timescale

It is helpful to both child and primary caregiver to have an idea how long the treatment work is likely to last. The child or young person may be being considered for a groupwork programme that runs for a set number of sessions, or for a more open-ended contract of individual work. Either way, there should be some idea about what level of commitment is being asked for from both the child, who will be attending, and the primary caregiver, who may be accompanying. Sometimes open-ended work can seem too threatening. A limited number of sessions can feel too rushed. The younger the child, the more a focused and time-limited approach may be appropriate. As a primary caregiver, you can help by discussing what you think would best suit your child.

Expectations

It is important for expectations to be clear at the outset. Clearly, for younger children it is essential that they are accompanied to each session and picked up at the end, preferably by the same person. Adolescents may want to go on their own but they will need to demonstrate to the adults who care for them that they can do so responsibly. This means arriving on time and returning home safely. The primary caregiver, the helper and any other protecting adults need to check with one another that this is happening. Some young people may leave and return on time but not actually go to their sessions.

Clearly, there is also the expectation that the child or young person will attend the sessions regularly and will cancel appointments in advance if they are unable to attend. For anyone accompanying a child or young person to appointments, the travelling to and from the sessions is often a time for additional discussion. This can be very positive and emphasises the important role that the accompanying person plays in the child's recovery process.

A professional helper should let you know that the situation will improve and give you an idea of the likely process. As mentioned earlier, once the child begins to discuss the sexual abuse, it is extremely common that difficult behaviours will get worse before they get better.

If there is a serious doubt about the likelihood of improvement, this should be discussed openly at the outset. This is rare but does occur, as in situations where a child requires very intensive work but resources are not available. In that case, the work offered is not the best form of treatment, but is all that is available. This may mean that the outcome will not be as good as was hoped for.

Some children and young people are so distressed that it is unclear at the outset what type of treatment will be useful for them. They may also be so out of control themselves that they will not be able to use treatment at this time. They may be acting out sexually by sexually abusing other children; they may be sniffing glue, drinking alcohol or taking drugs; or they might be self-harming or overdosing. These very extreme behaviours call for specialist resources. These children are much more likely to require residential placements rather than weekly one-to-one sessions, and may also need to be assessed by a child psychologist or psychiatrist.

If these children are living at home, the primary caregiver, as well as the young person, will need a lot of support. If the child is placed in a residential unit, the expectations the unit has of the primary caregiver should be made clear. Some units involve families and friends actively in their recovery programmes for residents. Some also like children and young people to return home at weekends.

All professional workers involved in caring for children and young people are expected to behave professionally towards them. It is gross professional misconduct for any professional to hit or in any way physically abuse, to have sexual relations or in any way sexually harass, to verbally abuse or to humiliate any child or young person with whom they are working. If your child tells you about any improper professional conduct, take it seriously and report it immediately to the statutory safeguarding workers. Professional workers are paid to be protectors of children, and a breach of duty in this respect is totally unacceptable. Guidelines have been produced by various professional groups to monitor and maintain good practice.[1]

Criteria for termination

It is important to know if there are criteria for termination of the treatment work. It may be that the child or young person must attend a certain proportion of the sessions offered. They may also need to demonstrate an ability to use the sessions. If they spend every session in silence or refuse to participate, it is unlikely to be a beneficial experience in the long run. It is often difficult for children to refuse treatment when adults who care for them are extremely keen they should have it. Often the only way to express their dissatisfaction is to refuse to participate in the session itself.

On a more positive note, how will everyone know that the time has come to finish the work, especially if it is an open-ended contract? What are the signs or indicators that the child or young person has

---

1   So for my own discipline, you can find information on complaints at www.bps.org.uk/e-services/find-a-psychologist/complaints.cfm, or in a broader context, such as abuse in a residential unit, see www.whistleblowing.org.uk/index.htm.

recovered enough to no longer need professional input? It can be helpful to discuss this directly with the child or young person. Who decides when the work should finish, or if it should start again?

> **I know I would need help again if I started isolating myself again – or if I started to think about it all of the time. I don't now, so maybe it's over.**
> *Alison*

> **. . . I needed help again. I was always crying and everything and that was the first time I ran away. My social worker's boss thought I should go to one of them men you can go to and talk to . . . I don't get all the different names, like psychologists and psychiatrists . . . but I don't really want to go and see a man, I'd rather see the woman I saw before.**
> *Natasha*

If a child has had a good relationship with a previous therapist, and they feel they need additional help, it is best to see if that person is still available to offer help. The shared knowledge and experience often mean they can get down to sorting out the current difficulty more quickly.

If the previous therapist is not available, the child or young person may have clear ideas about who or what kind of therapy they would find useful. Natasha was clear she wanted to see a woman. A clear preference should be respected.

Termination of a particular treatment does not necessarily mean that all therapy has to stop. If one type of treatment, for example, group work, doesn't appear to be helping, another type, such as one-to-one work, can be tried; if the child or the therapist cannot continue because someone is moving, new therapists can be found.

Abrupt endings should be avoided. Both the primary caregiver and the child should know when the work is scheduled to finish. The ending should be positive, leaving the child or young person feeling they can manage or that arrangements have been made to find someone else to carry on.

Evaluation of change

It is useful at the outset of treatment work to think about the signs that will indicate that your child is beginning to recover from their experience of sexual abuse. You may want to discuss this with the professional helper. If a primary caregiver is specifically looking for symptom reduction, then clearly they will think treatment work is finished when the distressing behaviours have gone. Not all professional helpers would see the reduction of symptoms as an indication that treatment work can finish. So it is important for everyone to be clear why the work is being undertaken, what will be discussed and when the work will end. Professional helpers should be able to explain why they work the way they do and what benefits the child will gain.

Other treatment issues

It is important that primary caregivers are involved at the outset of therapeutic work, if only to meet the professional worker, but if an adolescent makes the referral themselves, that would not be appropriate. Children and young people may also use telephone helplines to help them recover. Even if the primary caregiver comes to know about this, it would not be appropriate for them to interfere.

Consideration needs to be given to the gender and ethnicity of the professional helper. Many children, especially adolescents, are very sensitive about gender and express a clear preference for working with women (particularly, of course, if they have been sexually abused by men). For children from minority ethnic families, a professional helper from the same ethnic group is preferable. If this is not possible, it is important that the professional helper has a clear understanding of the limits of their cultural knowledge. Where the child and the professional helper are from the same community, it is important that issues regarding confidentiality are clearly spelt out.

Where it has not been possible to provide children or young people with a professional helper who meets all of their requirements regarding ethnicity and gender, it is important to discuss this at the beginning of the work and recognise that there may be aspects of the experience that will be especially difficult or even impossible to share.

Treatment work should not cause further harm to the child or young person. Consequently, attention needs to be paid to the timing of the offer of treatment as well as to the fit between professional and client. It may be helpful for a child to have a break between different pieces of treatment work so that they can consolidate gains. For example, they may have just finished a group or family work when they are referred for individual work. An uninterrupted stream of treatment work can be counter-therapeutic in that it becomes the habitual way of dealing with problems. It can also undermine the natural healing network that surrounds every child by not actively incorporating the child's surrounding network into the recovery process.

If, as a primary caregiver, you feel the treatment is doing more harm than good, it is very important to discuss this with the professional helper as soon as possible.

If a child or young person clearly does not want to continue with their treatment work, it would be wrong to force them. With younger children, the primary caregiver can discuss the issue with the professional helper. With adolescents, it can be hard to find the balance between speaking for them and letting them find their own voice.

In an earlier example, Natasha expressed a clear preference for working with a woman after being referred to a man.

Q: Were you able to say that?
Natasha: *No, I didn't say nothing 'cause, like, she [the team leader] was doing most of the talking.*

Q: Did you think about asking to see the woman you saw before?
Natasha: *No, I was thinking about it but I was scared to say anything.*

In this situation, Natasha needed someone to be her advocate. She knew she needed more help and had a clear idea who might be able to help. The professional workers heard part of her message – "I need help" – but then moved too quickly into providing a helper without considering that Natasha might have some ideas about what kind of help she wanted based on her previous experiences of therapy.

Goals of treatment work

Treatment work should help the child or young person and their primary caregiver achieve a sense of mastery over an experience that violated them and took away their sense of control.

> I think [therapy] really helped me, like, come to terms with the fact that I was abused – that other people do it but you can get over it in the end. It helped me share my feelings, like, half the time I didn't have to say 'cause, like, [my helper] knew. It was as though she was a mind reader and really knew what would help me . . . She thought of the best way possible of bringing that out – of helping . . . she used pictures, she wrote that song . . . I still got bits of that song everywhere[2] . . . She helped me come to terms with the fact that it wasn't

2   'My body's nobody's body but mine; you run your own body, let me run mine', from the song *Feeling Yes Feeling No*.

> my fault; that it happens to other people; that you can
> be helped, that you can get over it and you can start
> afresh and, like, you don't always have to be living in
> the past – living with that cloud over your head saying
> "It can happen again".
> *Natasha*

Treatment work should convey to the child or young person a strong
sense of being believed. It should affirm their feelings, whatever
they may be, and help them explore feelings that are less
comfortable and maybe even scary. It should increase their self-
esteem. To help the recovery process, it is important that the issue
of responsibility for the sexual abuse is explored, starting from the
premise that adults have a responsibility to protect and *not* abuse.
It is important that the child's sense of blame is addressed that,
regardless of the fact that the strategies they used for protecting
themselves are often interpreted as contributing to the abuse, they
are not to blame for what happened.

It is important to recognise and name the survival tactics they
employed. It can help a young person immensely to view something
like bed-wetting as a survival tactic. It may now be a habit, but it
may once have been the most effective way of terminating an
episode of sexual abuse.

It is essential to help the child, young person or primary caregiver
identify triggers for challenging or out-of-control behaviour. Giving
the child a sense of mastery or control means they must be able to
recognise when they might lose control, and learn other ways of
coping with the feelings that are triggered. There are many different
ways for this to be achieved – either in work with a professional or
with the primary caregiver.

> Blanking out just happens and I don't always know why
> it has happened. [In one way] it is good, because it

helps me to say what I want without getting any
emotion or memory of saying it. Now that it has been
pointed out to me that I do it, I can see that I used to
do it before, especially when I was with him.
Lisa

Different types of work to help children heal

Treatment work can be offered on a one-to-one basis, in groups or
with other family members. Sometimes a combination of all three is
useful. All of the issues laid out earlier in this chapter regarding the
setting up in advance of clear ways of working are relevant,
regardless of what type of treatment is offered.

Family work

Working together as a family can be helpful.[3] Sexual abuse is
something that distorts family life by promoting an atmosphere of
secrecy and dishonesty. If, during and after the investigation, a
family member is excluded from the family home, this will have a
profound effect on all family members. It is important that the
family can discuss this with an outsider, who should be more able
to raise some of the difficult issues.

Offering help to all family members may make it easier for the child
who was targeted to use their treatment time. For example, in a
follow-up of young women who attended a group-work
programme, the issue of additional help for other family members
was raised (Smith, 1992). The young women made a number of
points and comments about their experience and views:

- I felt guilty that only I got offered groups.
- My brother is very blocked about it. He felt he let me down. He's

---

3   The Association for Family Therapy helps families to find a trained family therapist in
    their area; see www.aft.org.uk.

been different to me ever since. He's never hugged me or comforted me. He was so important to me. I looked up to him.
- I think groups for mums would have made me feel better, knowing she was getting help too.

Of the 14 young women interviewed, five said it would have been helpful if their mothers had been offered help; four specifically mentioned their brothers; and one specifically mentioned how unhelpful she had found family work because the perpetrator was also present (Smith, 1992).

If a family is referred for treatment, the perpetrator should not be included, unless he has had considerable treatment himself and the child whom he abused is ready for this to happen (Morrison *et al*, 1994).

Group work

Having the opportunity to discuss issues in groups with others who have shared a similar experience is a good way of practising the far harder task of talking with one's own family. All of the young women followed up for the evaluation mentioned above thought the groups were useful. They all thought it was most valuable because it broke down the isolation they felt (Smith, 1992).

> Instead of, like, you just being by yourself, it's like you have to come up with all the answers – everyone puts in answers and everyone works together . . .
> *Natasha*

> The group gives you a chance to talk about your feelings with someone else who's been through it . . . we'd all have to listen to each other.
> *Alison*

A group-work experience should help individuals feel connected to others who have shared a similar experience. It can be helpful to make sure this will happen by checking out some basic information about important issues such as the ethnic mix of the group.

In the girls' group follow-up, one young white woman remarked, 'There was only one "coloured girl" and she didn't come very often'. It may have been that being the only black girl in a group of white girls did not help the young woman feel less alone but rather emphasised her isolation from her community. Contrast this with Alison's more culturally mixed group-work experience.

> **The group itself was mixed racially. The group leaders were two women – one was Indian and one was black. The group really helped. We talked about it – they knew a lot . . . the women who ran the group – they were really good. Before the group I sort of felt I was the only one.**
> *Alison*

If your child has a disability, hopefully at least one other group member will too. A very different experience from the rest of the group or something that sets one member apart will need to be handled very carefully in a group setting. If your child is different from others in the group in any way, it may be advisable for you to decide to ask for one-to-one work instead.

It can be helpful to find out if there are any local groups. These groups may be run by professionals or they may function as self-help groups. Remember that some of the issues to think about when looking for professional help for your child are just as important when using a self-help network.

If the group-work programme has an outline of the topics covered, it can be useful for primary caregivers to have these. They can then follow up or watch for particular signs of distress after certain sessions. Many group-work programmes often run parallel caregiver groups.

Individual work

Most of this chapter has been addressing issues in relation to one-to-one work. This is perhaps what is most likely to be offered if you seek professional help. One-to-one work can range from counselling and play therapy sessions to individual psychotherapy.[4] There is a wide variety of approaches, so it is helpful to ask questions about the work as outlined in the previous section.

If you don't like what your child has been offered, you can refuse treatment. Clearly the central role of the therapist in one-to-one work emphasises the need for you to trust this person to help your child. In group or family work there are other people who also play a crucial role in the healing process and the importance of the individual therapist is less crucial.

Sometimes a child or young person cannot work with the professional who has been assigned to help. It can be difficult to raise this but it may be crucial for you and the child, as well as being important feedback for the professional. The issues of gender and ethnicity are again more potent in one-to-one work. If you or the child have any doubts or reservations about the work, these should be raised at an initial meeting. It may be helpful to start with a limited number of sessions and review how these have gone before committing yourself and the child to a protracted piece of therapeutic work.

Some of the issues that may come up in both individual and group settings relate to the child's feelings towards the perpetrator, their non-abusing parent and their siblings. Often they feel unable initially to discuss these in a family context. Having their own space to air these feelings is very important.

---

4   UKCP (UK Council for Psychotherapy) registers child psychotherapists. Other creative therapies like art therapy, drama therapy and play therapy have their own registering bodies. Check that the person you are working with is registered with a professional body. This ensures they have been trained to a standard and operate with a code of ethical practice.

Managing challenging behaviours

Many children who have been sexually abused display challenging behaviour even after the sexual abuse itself has stopped. In part, this may be because they still feel unsafe. It is also likely that they will be having unwanted memories or flashbacks to the experience of sexual abuse, which will trigger the challenging behaviour.

> When I listen to certain music it reminds me of him and what he did to me. I feel really high and out of it. It is almost as if I'm in a world of my own – sort of blanked out – which is what I did when he abused me. I'm not in control of my actions, I feel really weird, as if anything could happen and it wouldn't affect me. And I don't care who sees me or what they think of me or what I'm doing. At these times I'm most likely to cut up or drink myself silly.
> *Lisa*

It can be helpful to remind yourself that some of these behaviours helped the child or young person to cope with the experience of sexual abuse. In Lisa's case, the blanking out helped her endure what her abuser did to her. Now when she blanks out, she hurts herself.

Until you can teach or help the child to find other ways of dealing with their distress, they are likely to carry on with the challenging and often disturbing behaviour. You may see a clear pattern to the behaviour. There may be specific triggers – similarities that remind the child of their experience of sexual abuse. For example, whenever Natasha saw her mother on contact visits, her eczema always got worse. To help you identify possible triggers to unwanted memories, think of dates; time of day; all of the five senses – seeing, hearing, smelling, touching, tasting; certain situations; certain types of people; or certain feelings.

> Sometimes, when I get angry or upset, you know – it
> comes back . . . or when you read these sorts of things
> in the paper.
> *Alison*

In one-to-one work, Lisa made the following list of things that still
brought back memories for her:

- Cortinas
- Capital Radio/Radio 1
- pink jumper
- metal case full of bits
- dole forms (UB40)
- blue eyes, blond hair, tall, skinny, beer gut
- jeans, blue jumper
- Ribena cartons
- tissues
- a long list of dates and specific places.

It can be helpful to think of things to do that reduce the negative
consequences of the triggers. In many cases, primary caregivers and
the child or young person themselves do not recognise the triggers,
and the behaviours that follow are often very negative and
destructive.

> I like to cut myself because I get so frustrated that I
> don't know what to do with the anger and upset inside
> me. Also to make myself look uglier so that it will
> never happen again.
> *Lisa*

Helping Lisa identify what made her angry was part of disrupting
the pattern of her self-harming.

Sometimes there is a context in which problem behaviours are
appropriate. But with self-harming, there is no acceptable context.
Lisa was helped not only to identify triggers but also to find

something else to do when she felt frustrated, angry and upset. She was also reassured that her appearance was not what caused the sexual abuse.

Ten-year-old David used to get very upset and then urinate in his bedroom. His mother was able to connect the urination on the carpet with his fear and upset following his experience of sexual abuse by his stepfather. She talked to him about his feelings and put a bucket in his room. She told him if he was worried and upset but unable to come out of his room at night he could urinate in the bucket. Every day she would clean the bucket. If he had used it the night before, she made a safe time for him to talk about what had scared or upset him. Gradually he used the bucket less and less, and talked with his mother more and more.

David's mother made it possible for him to express his feelings in a safer and, literally, more contained fashion. She recognised that he was still not able to put some of his feelings about his experience of sexual abuse into words. She provided him with an alternative and followed up with safe time to talk about his worries. She understood that using the bucket at night was a signal to her that he had something to say but needed her help to say it.

Sometimes primary caregivers will need to discuss ways of managing challenging behaviour with a professional helper. Together they may identify the triggers for it and provide alternatives for the child or young person that make them feel more in charge or in control of themselves and their feelings.

If, as a protecting parent, there are now episodes of behaviour you see in a different light, it is important that you share this with your child. It is important for them to know that you did notice certain behaviours but that you incorrectly assumed they meant something else. For example, Asha, whose stepfather sexually abused her, found that if she slept in her sister's bed with her sister he would leave her alone. Her mother noticed Asha's requests to sleep with her sister and thought it odd because they seemed to fight so much when they were together. After a while, she encouraged Asha to be grown up and sleep in her own bed. It never occurred to her that Asha slept in her sister's bed to escape being sexually abused.

Treatment work with protecting primary caregivers and children should go a long way towards resolving the emotional consequences of sexual abuse, as identified in Chapter 5. However, there are times when specific, additional pieces of work may need to be done, such as preparing children for legal proceedings or helping children move to alternative families or residential units. These may be time-limited pieces of work with a clear focus and end point in mind.

Conclusion

The healing process begins with the disclosure or discovery that sexual abuse is happening. The consequences of the experience often lead to periods of time when the child is distressed and unable to get on with age-appropriate tasks. In these cases it may be necessary to seek professional help. This doesn't mean you have failed your child because you can't make things better. It underlines your commitment to sort out the difficulties and use whatever help you can to do it.

Specialist resources are scarce, and the information in this chapter should help protecting adults become more aware of those resources so that their children can get the best from them. It is very important that professionals work closely with primary caregivers, to make best use of each other in order to maximise the potential for healing. Useful resources and addresses are included in the Appendix.

Healing and recovery work can happen in different ways and places, not just with a professional therapist. Remember you are teaching your child to learn to take care of themselves, to be able to get help when they need it and to use it effectively.

Sexual abuse need not dominate someone's life forever, especially if it has been stopped. The healing process should aim to put the experience of sexual abuse into a wider context and life experience – one which allows the individual to develop their potential and to express themselves without fear of disbelief but with the courage it takes to survive.

References

Morrison T, Erooga M and Beckett R (eds) (1994) *Sexual Offending Against Children: Assessment and treatment of male abusers*, London: Routledge

Smith G (1992) *Thamesmead Girls Group Evaluation* (unpublished report to Greenwich ACPC), London: Greenwich ACPC

7

Sexual abuse and trauma

We can easily underestimate the traumatic elements of a child's experience of sexual abuse by not seeing it from the child's point of view. Remember when Jay described the violence and abuse he witnessed (see pp.101–2) and experienced and stated, 'That's when I died'. He described many serious episodes, but his statement 'That's when I died' indicates that this particular episode was a "near death experience" for him. Of course, it is clear to us as adults that he did not die, but what the child is describing is *their* experience of the event. This needs to be recognised and taken seriously in helping him to understand what has happened to him. Feeling you are going to die or that you died would qualify as a traumatic event. Many young children have not yet developed sophisticated concepts of death and can report, as Jay did, a previous death which is factually not correct, but was experienced psychologically. This is what trauma is all about – an overwhelming experience where you feel that your survival is threatened.

In recognising that sexual abuse is often embedded in other adverse childhood experiences, we need to understand the dynamics of trauma and how to help a child recover from traumatic experiences. Much of what is presented here arises from the clinical practice in the Child and Adolescent Mental Health Service for Looked After Children based at Alder Hey Children's Hospital, Liverpool. This is a trauma-based service that views looked after children's experiences of significant harm as traumatic events rather than as mental illnesses or psychiatric conditions. We also work with primary caregivers to help create a context of recovery around the child – whether that is in a residential unit, a foster placement, a kinship care placement or their family of origin.

Unlike single traumatic events, sexual abuse is part of a process that is rooted in relationships, passes through ambiguous interactions and moves to more overtly sexually inappropriate ones. Because it happens in a family context, it may not be only the child who is traumatised. We also have a better understanding of the trans-generational aspects of trauma. A mother who was abused as a child may be overly protective of her children as a consequence of her experiences. She may inadvertently foster an atmosphere of mistrust and fear regarding the wider world to her child. Her children may show hyper-vigilance as a consequence without having ever been abused themselves.

This book focuses on working with children but they need to be understood in the context of their family of origin, foster family or residential unit. As sexual abuse is an abuse of relationship, it is likely to lead to distorted family relationships even after the abuse has stopped. This is similar to situations where there has been domestic violence. The perpetrator may leave, but the legacy of coercive control may remain.

Many parents and foster carers notice something different about the child in certain agitated states. Some describe it 'like a mist coming down' or 'a look in their eyes'. It is possible they are describing a child who is in a traumatised state where they are reliving their past traumatic experiences. At that time, the child is not able to differentiate between past and present. They are not able to use all of their brain and may be driven by the midbrain – the feeling centre of the brain (a simple description of the evolution of the brain is given in Chilton Pearce, 2002). In a non-traumatised individual, the brain works in an integrated fashion. However, when someone has been traumatised, the different parts of their brain begin to work separately from time to time when triggered by reminders of traumatic events. Often this is in a more primitive manner, based on survival. The primitive brain tends to focus on either approach or avoidance. This is often referred to as the "fight or flight" mode. This can be seen frequently in children and young people who have been traumatised by experiences of sexual abuse. This cut-off state of mind is often observed by primary caregivers, who may have found it difficult to deal with because usual techniques like distraction or talking don't seem to work.

Having a basic understanding about trauma and its effects can be helpful in managing a child's behaviour.[1] Our service runs an active teaching programme that incorporates a number of key concepts, including an understanding of the traumatic process.

Recognising and responding to the traumatic aspects of sexual abuse are an important part of the recovery process, especially as sexual abuse rarely occurs in isolation but is accompanied by many other adverse childhood experiences. It is crucial to keep this in mind when working with a child who has been sexually abused. As a parent you are likely to be overwhelmed as well, which is why external help may be necessary. This can also be true for kinship carers because the issues will touch them personally, unlike for foster carers who have no prior relationship with the child, or the perpetrator for that matter.

Remember that the child is likely to have been silenced by threats of violence to themselves or their loved ones, including pets. They will be made to feel worthless and ashamed of their participation. They will have been induced to feel guilty and partly responsible. They can also feel consumed with anger, sometimes murderous rage. They may be frightened of talking about the abuse because when they do they begin to re-experience it all over again.

---

1   For information regarding childhood trauma, go to www.childtraumaacademy.com.

> **Maybe he has spent time stuck in a cell but that will
> never make up for what was done to me . . . the judge
> who put him away didn't put him away for long
> enough as far as I'm concerned. I just got so much
> anger inside me for him. It's almost like he committed
> the crime but I have to suffer for it . . . I'm scared that
> he will come after me and start threatening me.**
> *Lisa*

In helping a child to recover, you need to remind yourself and the
child that they have been manipulated into keeping the abuse secret
and feeling like an equal participant. If they were involved in
recruiting others, this needs to be put into the context of abusive
environments and survival tactics. This applies also to children who
have abused younger siblings. Helping children develop self-talk that
addresses some of these issues can be helpful.

Kay had been abused within her family of origin. This involved many
adults and children. Kay was encouraged to behave sexually with
her siblings. When she came for therapy she was very sexualised.
She developed a conversation that helped her to control some of
her sexual feelings.

> **My brain is in charge of my whole body. If my private
> parts tell me to do something, I can choose not to.**

This intervention was part of a number of different strategies put in
place to help Kay with her feelings. Being able to label them,
understand where in her body she felt them and how she might
manage them was part of her treatment programme. Traumatic
sexual experiences can lead to sexualised responses becoming the
habitual way to respond to any stressful event. It can also interfere
with the labelling of emotions.

Children can be further traumatised by the investigative procedures.
It was not the investigators' intention to cause further upset but the
examples below, seen from the child's point of view, convey how

frightening and disturbing the investigative process can be.

> I think the worst bit that I didn't like was my mum and
> my dad in the same room. It was like, 'Oh, no . . . ' At
> one or two points . . . my dad was in the same room
> when they were talking and the dolls were in the bag
> on the side [and I thought] they'll say something . . .
> I was scared of that.
> *Natasha*

Natasha is describing when she was interviewed by the police.
At that time people thought it was only her stepfather who had
abused her, but over time it was clear that her father had also
sexually abused her and Natasha had witnessed her mother sexually
abusing her brother.

> I felt really dirty. I felt embarrassed saying what had
> happened. [The police] were okay. They were really nice
> – [they explained things to me] and that's when it hit
> me. I thought, 'Oh, God, what have I done?' They took
> a statement off of me. And then it was just all solicitors
> and social workers . . .
> *Alison*

You can see that Alison thought she had done something wrong.
She may also have been wondering if telling was the right thing to
do because many professionals had then become involved. In her
case, the criminal conviction failed on a technicality.

> At the trial, when they found out about what
> happened – Mum wouldn't let me go – they came back
> and told me. I just couldn't believe it. My social worker
> was just sitting there and she didn't know what to say
> really, and my mum – she was angry . . . I just couldn't
> believe it . . . He got away with it. The policewoman
> who took my statement – when I gave her a day, she
> looked back on the calendar and got the wrong date so

> we lost the case . . . just because of one date I lost the whole thing, just like that.
> *Alison*

The medical examination can also be traumatising and likely to bring back bad memories.

> I went downstairs into this other place . . . they wanted to check me to make sure nothing was wrong . . . I remember this man and rubber gloves and I was just thinking, 'Oh, my God, what is he going to do?' And, like, he checked out my privates and I was just thinking, 'Oh no no no, I want to get out, I want to get out'.
> *Natasha*

An introduction to sexual intimacy via a sexually abusive interaction is never going to be a positive experience, and can be described as traumatic sexualisation. The child's sexual feelings and sexual identity are likely to be shaped in an inappropriate and interpersonally dysfunctional way. While they may go through a period where sexual intimacy is not a focus of social interaction, sexuality and sexual intimacy will be part of adolescent experience. Sometimes traumatic flashbacks occur in those sexually intimate relationships. The young person can also experience dissociative states.

Dissociative tendencies are an enduring response to trauma. When a child enters a dissociative state, they no longer retain the capacity to reflect concurrently on their actions, thoughts and feelings. This means they cannot independently modulate their feelings during the event. Newborn babies similarly depend on their primary caregiver to help them modulate their feelings – like hunger, pain, tiredness, discomfort and excitement. It may be helpful to reflect on a child's early experiences for clues as to why they cannot manage their feelings now. Many children in the care system will not have been cared for in an attentive and responsive manner. Very basic needs to be fed, to go to sleep or to be comforted will not have been met.

The child will not see adults as sources of comfort.

As the child's normal memory systems are inaccessible at times of high stress (and this can include being excited positively rather than only fearfully), they often have little or no recall – and what is available to them is fragmented. Memories of the traumatic events are often of an intrusive type commonly considered to be "flashbacks". Children often re-enact their traumatic experiences through play, nightmares or repetitive conversations.

Kiera meticulously recorded her daughter Jasmine's behaviour following the supervised weekly contact until the matter of the sexual abuse was resolved in court. The court ordered an assessment to take place and contact was suspended until the assessment was complete. Jasmine's symptomatic behaviour – including fearfulness, bed-wetting and compulsive masturbation – reduced dramatically over the time of the suspended contact. As part of the assessment, Jasmine was ordered to see her father. Following this visit, Jasmine's symptomatic behaviour returned. She began to wet the bed and masturbate and it took two weeks for these behaviours to subside. The meticulous record-keeping was vital in establishing the link between Jasmine's symptomatic behaviour and contact with her father. On the basis of this, as well as the other evidence presented, it was possible to recommend a cessation of contact until such time as Jasmine could protect herself and express her own views. At the time the ruling was made, Jasmine was only four.

The following extracts from Kiera's diary show how traumatised Jasmine was and the efforts she made to make sense of Jasmine's experience. It also clearly demonstrates traumatic triggers for Jasmine. Discussions about her father trigger episodes of self-harming and sexualised behaviours. Her nightie is a trigger to memories of being touched on her bottom. It also shows how Jasmine is trying to resist by saying no and being ignored. Tina is Jasmine's aunt.

13 May

J asked to see Daddy. Tina said do you want to? J replied no – don't like him. Tina asked why, what does Daddy do? J said he hurts me, he hits me on my back and on my tummy and pats my boo boos. During the conversation she kept trying to touch her boobs and look down her top. Got in a temper a few times, keeps hitting herself and saying she doesn't like and love herself.

14 May

While getting J into her nightie she said he's not hurting me. Tina said who? J said Daddy. T said why? J said Daddy hurts me in this nightie. Tina asked what does Daddy do. J said he pulls it and touches my bottom. Tina asked what J did. J said I said no and Daddy cried.

7 August

Didn't wet bed. When getting ready in bathroom, asked if her Daddy would hurt her when she saw him. I said no. She said I ask him not to.

7 November

Wet bed. Not too bad. Still hitting herself on the head. Had a dream during the night. Woke up crying. Asked her what the dream was about. J said frightened. Daddy at my window. Came in my bedroom. Restless all night, just wanted me to cuddle her.

These recordings give a clear picture of the child's distress. They also show a child who is being re-traumatised by continuing contact with someone she fears. Often, frequent contact with a fearful parental figure exacerbates the child's traumatic responses and increases their symptomatic behaviours. Natasha was older and more able to express her views.

> I went to see the judge and I saw the court that it
> happened in . . . she tried her best to explain to me that
> they ask, like, my mum questions . . . they were making
> decisions that I shouldn't live with my mum, and that I'll
> get contact once a week and that was changed to every
> two weeks, and then monthly. And then 'cause [the
> contact] kept getting me upset, my social worker went
> to the judge and got it stopped.
> *Natasha*

Repeated exposure to feared stimuli with no way of avoiding it is
likely to lead to increased traumatic responses. This could be
extreme acting out, dissociative responses, nightmares, soiling and
wetting. It is likely that if these symptoms are ignored they will
become worse and possibly disrupt and/or severely stress a foster
placement.

If you find yourself in a situation where you have to support a
contact arrangement that is clearly stressful for your child, think of
ways you can reduce that stress. It can help if you:

- are physically present;
- travel with the child to and from their contact;
- talk about it before or after;
- reassure the child as much as you can;
- help them think how they could make the contact go better.

> It can feel like a betrayal of the child to take them to
> contact when they so clearly don't want to go or find it
> so stressful. It is important to explain to your child that
> it isn't your decision to send them on access visits (even
> if supervised). Try to explain and comfort them when
> they are upset about going. Reassure them it isn't your
> decision.
> *Kiera*

When a child or young person's memory is fragmented by their traumatic experiences, it is hard to work with them therapeutically. Often what they say or how they behave is devoid of emotional content. This can be very disturbing for primary caregivers and sometimes lead them to believe that the sexual abuse did not happen. In these cases, a containing therapeutic environment is essential to commence meaningful work on traumatic behaviours. Parents and foster carers are likely to need specialist input, support and guidance to help them manage not only the child's feelings but also their own.

Piecemeal interventions, such as anger management or play therapy, are likely to be insufficient to support the placement. The child or young person needs to experience the benefits of a reparative family experience. This involves seeing non-abusing parents as resources and sources of comfort.

In general, when working with children who have been traumatised, it is important to address a number of key issues. Working through primary caregivers is likely to provide a stronger therapeutic response, because the primary caregiver can modify and amend interventions for a particular child based on their knowledge of that child. They will also have more opportunities to deliver interventions in the course of day-to-day events. At CAMHS, we work towards:

- enhancing the skills and competence of primary caregivers;
- increasing the bond between the child and their primary caregiver through nurturing, healing touch;
- increasing the potency of the primary caregiver as a resource for the child when he or she is agitated;
- reducing the risk of secondary post-traumatic stress disorder (PTSD) for carers by identifying recovery tasks for them to participate in as a form of restitution and reparation for the damaged relationship between adult/parent and their child;
- reducing the child's hyper-arousal through breath awareness and physical activities aimed at improving left–right co-ordination – for example, a martial art or playing a musical instrument;
- creating a coherent narrative of the traumatic event for the child

and their primary caregiver;
- increasing the child's self-efficacy through developmentally appropriate self-care tasks and specific tasks focused on caring for others;
- screening for extreme cases of PTSD that may need direct intervention such as CBT or EMDR;[2]
- intervention based on the child's neurobiological development aimed at bypassing verbal interventions through the use of other non-verbal therapeutic interventions such as music, art, and movement.

It is important to help the child to understand their abusive and traumatic experience. This means hearing the "relevant account",[3] which may not be the sexual abuse. Remember that when Jay spoke about his experiences (see pp.101–2) he described his father's violence to his mother first. In trauma work, you often work through layers. This can be, and I think is, part of life story work. It should focus on helping the child develop a coherent narrative about their lived experience (Vetere and Dowling, 2005; Smith, 2005).

Within this work it is important to increase the child's repertoire of self so that they begin to see themselves as more than a sex object, for example. It may be important to help them think about gender issues, as both boys and girls from abusive families frequently start to develop very negative and restrictive stories about men in general and fathers in particular.

We use a range of modalities to treat the child, not only in terms of group, family or individual work but also by using all of the senses – visual, aural, olfactory and tactile. We work increasingly with the breath – helping primary carers focus on their own breathing and in turn that of the child or young person. This forms one of the basic building blocks of our Self Soothing Course (Smith and Lewis, 2007).

---

2   CBT (cognitive behaviour therapy) and EMDR (Eye Movement Desensitisation & Reprocessing – www.emdr.org.uk) are two treatments recommended in the NICE guidelines (www.nice.org.uk).

3   This I have borrowed form Elsa Jones, who wrote about adult survivors of abuse.

The course was devised because of a recognition that self-soothing or affect regulation is a skill lacking in many traumatised children, who can become addicted to high levels of stress. The research on the impact of chronic stress on overall physical health is convincing in terms of the negative consequences (Felitti *et al*, 1998).[4]

Of course there is no magic wand, but we do use imagination, creativity and play when working with children and young people (Charnock and Smith, 2005; Smith and Lewis, 2007).[5] This runs alongside psycho-educational information about trauma generally but applied specifically in relation to a particular child. We help primary caregivers predict and manage traumatic triggers for their child and provide clearly defined strategies for managing them at home.

It is essential that the primary caregiver remains psychologically available, and we encourage consistency, predictability and reliability. We help primary caregivers understand that this is a re-parenting experience. It will require repetition before the child comes to understand and respond to these characteristics in a more predictable, reliable and consistent manner themselves.

Because many abusive family situations are based on coercive control, we encourage primary caregivers to use negotiation and co-operation as their primary parental strategies. This can be difficult because the child or young person is not used to adults behaving like this and may try to encourage a bullying, intimidating and threatening atmosphere within the new home environment (if they have been placed) or maintaining the previously threatening environment because it is familiar.

Re-parenting a child or young person who has been traumatised requires a high level of self-awareness. They will challenge many

---

4   This seminal paper has led to a significant amount of follow-up research, which can be found at www.acestudy.org.

5   *Art creativity and mental health* is a course we run in conjunction with Tate Liverpool (see also Smith and Lewis, 2007). It is offered to foster carers and residential workers and involves the exhibitions in the gallery and a trip with a looked after child to the gallery.

assumptions you have about family life and require explanations about simple things you may have taken for granted. For example, Kay was certain her foster dad didn't sexually abuse her only because her foster mother wouldn't let him. She needed to be told he was not sexually interested in little girls and that he was in control of his own behaviour.

It is important if you are working as a two-parent family that you remain a cohesive system; we request that couples attend together to facilitate this. We receive very positive feedback, but specifically from male caregivers who develop a clear understanding of their role as a male primary caregiver in the healing process.

We encourage primary caregivers to see the work that they do as primarily healing. By this we mean that it attempts to be:

- restorative – by attending to the abuse specifically and acknowledging the hurt and injustice to the child/young person that arises from abusive interactions;
- remedial – by correcting inappropriate messages;
- curative – by attending to the child/young person holistically, and specifically addressing problem areas/symptomatic behaviours;
- beneficial – by promoting the child/young person's best interests (McGuire, 2008).

In formulating treatment packages, we consider the age and developmental stage of the child. We have used a Developmental Wheel that bears some similarities to Patricia Crittenden's Dynamic Maturational Model.[6] We are always mindful of the degree of threat to the child and place the child's safety in the centre of our thinking. We consider the disruption of social and family networks regardless of whether the child is removed from their family of origin. Clearly, coming into care causes major disruptions to the child's social and family networks.

---

6   See www.patcrittenden.com/.

We assess the number, nature and pattern of traumatic events. It is likely there will be a number of traumatic events, not just one episode of sexual abuse. A model of complex post-traumatic stress is more effective in understanding the multiple stressors a child or young person will have been subjected to. We aim to provide early intervention, as this is more likely to produce beneficial changes for the child. Once problems become entrenched and a child is seriously distressed, it becomes more difficult to provide a containing environment to address the difficulties. Treatment Foster Care[7] is one attempt to address this issue. Multiple placements and moves increase the likelihood of a poor mental health outcome. By supporting primary caregivers, we hope to increase placement stability.

Research on the impact of trauma is unequivocal in terms of the consequences for children in the longer term. Traumatised children are likely to develop altered cardiovascular regulation and affective lability. This means they may have sudden and surprising mood changes and, once agitated, find it hard to calm down. They may show behavioural impulsivity – acting without thinking through the consequences. This can be the fight or flight response. They may have perceived a threat where there was none but they have learned better to respond quickly and take pre-emptive action, rather than risk something really bad happening. They show increased anxiety and coupled with that increased startle responses. Children and young people may find new situations hard to adapt to, and if interrupted unexpectedly or told something negative with no preparation, they may respond with an exaggerated and unmodulated negative response. They may have sleep abnormalities. These could take the form of regular night terrors, of which they are unaware, but almost certainly which their primary caregiver will know about. They may shout out in these night terrors or re-enact episodes that appear abusive. Seeing this is very upsetting for a primary caregiver. Night terrors are not the same as nightmares. They represent an aspect of trauma where the brain is trying to

---

7   Multidimensional Treatment Foster Care is described in *Every Child Matters: Change for children*. More information can be found at www.everychildmatters.gov.uk/socialcare/childrenincare/fostercare/mtfc.

process disturbing material but the experience is still not yet integrated – hence the reliving of the experience through the night terror. It is a kind of sleeping flashback.

The high levels of arousal the child or young person feels most often expresses itself through aggression – sometimes towards themself, sometimes towards others. It can also be the underlying reason for substance misuse – a form of self-medication.

It is also likely that traumatic experiences will have impacted on the child's capacity to pay attention. This may result in learning difficulties, because there are long periods of time when the child is dissociated. This combination of high levels of arousal and inability to pay attention can often be misdiagnosed as an Attention Deficit Disorder or Attention Deficit Hyperactivity Disorder (see Radcliffe and Newnes, 2005, for a detailed discussion of this issue).

Given all of these difficulties, it is not surprising for children who have been traumatised through the experience of sexual abuse to show attachment difficulties. They often have difficulties reading social cues and they may sexualise primary caregiving relationships. They are often disconnected from messages their bodies give them and respond to relationships through primitive midbrain responses of fight, flight, feeding and sexual approaches.

There is considerably more written about the impact of trauma that is beyond the scope of this book. As a caregiver, it is important for you to consider the issue of trauma in trying to understand your child's experience. This will help you arrange appropriate help for the child or young person. It will also help you to find support for yourself, to ensure that you do not develop secondary post-traumatic stress as a consequence of caring for a traumatised child.[8] It will also help you to find more strategies to aid your child's recovery process.

8   I am truly grateful to BAAF for allowing me and my colleague Sarah Borthwick, then a member of BAAF, to run a course on secondary PTSD for foster carers in 2000. The course programme remains unpublished.

References

Charnock V and Smith G (2005) 'Art creativity and mental health', in Smith G and Lewis S (2007) *Self Soothing Course: Dealing with everyday and extraordinary stress* (unpublished training manual), Alder Hey: Children's NHS Foundation Trust

Chilton Pearce J (2002) *The Biology of Transcendence: A blueprint of the human spirit*, Rochester, VT: Park Street Press

Felitti V, Anda R, Nordenberg D, Williamson D, Spitz A, Edwards V, Koss M and Marks J (1998) 'The relationship of adult health status to childhood abuse and household dysfunction', *American Journal of Preventive Medicine*, 14, pp. 245–58

McGuire F (2008) *Residential Support Programme* (unpublished), Alder Hey: Children's NHS Foundation Trust

Radcliffe N and Newnes C (eds) (2005) *Making and Breaking Children's Lives*, Ross-on-Wye: PCCS Books

Smith G (2005) 'Children's narratives of traumatic experiences', in Vetere A and Dowling E (eds) *Narrative Therapies with Children and their Families: A practitioner's guide to concepts and approaches*, New York, NY: Routledge

Smith G and Lewis S (2007) *Self Soothing Course: Dealing with everyday and extraordinary stress* (unpublished training manual), Alder Hey: Children's NHS Foundation Trust

Vetere A and Dowling E (eds) (2005) *Narrative Therapies with Children and their Families: A practitioner's guide to concepts and approaches*, New York, NY: Routledge

Afterword

For the children and protectors in this book, the responses to their disclosures of sexual abuse have been varied and often contradictory. Most of the children and young people are on the road to recovery because they have been believed and supported by enough protecting adults.

For **Natasha**, there was no criminal prosecution, but on balance of probability her sexual abuse by her father and stepfather was acknowledged in civil proceedings. Her mother was unable to accept this. As a consequence, Natasha has lived away from home in a foster family with her brother, David. She remained on a care order and had no contact with her family of origin. Natasha sought me out when she was 18 to talk about her experiences as a child. Her foster placement disrupted when she was about 15/16. There were a number of contributing factors, but one of the things Natasha said that stuck in my mind was that as her brother got older he looked more and more like their father, the man who had abused her. David had a significant learning difficulty that required intimate caregiving. She felt unable to do this, but also too guilty to tell anyone about the flashbacks she was having. She was living independently. When I worked with her, she was most interested in knowing what she was like as a little girl. I was pleased that I had saved some of her artwork and had good stories to tell about the work we had done together.

David was accommodated because his parents were unable to manage his care. He had severe epilepsy, which has caused physical and intellectual disabilities. He has very limited language. Like Natasha, he was sexually abused by his father and stepfather. However, he was also sexually abused by his mother, which Natasha witnessed. It was hard for Natasha to define this as sexual abuse for a number of reasons: it was what she had grown up with; David was unable to name his experience himself and Natasha was reluctant to do it for him; and sexual abuse by women is often harder to name for reasons relating to social expectations of women and their behaviour in relation to children. There were no criminal proceedings in connection with David's sexual abuse. The civil proceedings removing him from his family's care did not deal with allegations of sexual abuse because Natasha had not yet disclosed. She remained living at home until David's foster mother, whom Natasha saw regularly when visiting her brother, became concerned that Natasha may have been sexually abused. This activated the statutory child protection investigation that secured Natasha's safety and confirmed what the foster mother had thought. I think David's silent story of abuse is not unique – the unspoken abuse of children, young people and adults who are severely disabled and who will never tell their stories needs to be remembered and extra vigilance on our part is required. It is my hope that David remained in his safe and loving foster family and that his next move was overseen by people who loved him.

For **Alison**, there was a failed criminal prosecution. The perpetrator denied sexually abusing her, despite Alison's mother witnessing him doing so on one occasion. When she found her partner sexually abusing her daughter, Alison's mother contacted the police. Alison's mother believed everything her daughter told her. She terminated her relationship with her partner and Alison has remained at home with her mother and sister. I imagine Alison is a mother now –

certainly a beautiful young woman. I hope her relationship with her mother and younger sister continued to grow stronger and that together they have faced the world with the courage, love and strength they showed throughout the time I worked with them.

Lisa's perpetrator admitted sexually abusing her, but minimised both what he did and how long he had been doing it. He told the court he loved her and the local press reported the case sympathetically:

> This is not a case of an evil man – it is a case of a sexually naïve and immature man who *allowed his heart to rule his mind*. He was not motivated by evil or sexual gratification – he became emotionally and sexually attracted to her and *developed a boy/girl relationship*, albeit there was a great disparity in their ages [24 years]. A psychiatrist said [he] was *genuinely bewildered and remorseful* . . .

The material in italics in the above quote are explanations which were provided in court by professionals involved in defending Lisa's perpetrator and which were reported in the press. These professionals did not help Lisa's perpetrator to come to terms with what he had done and to get the help he would need if he were to stop sexually offending against children. The perpetrator's minimisations and distortions were acceptable to and supported by the wider professional system. In this case, the perpetrator admitted what he had done, which meant that Lisa did not have to prove that what she said was true. His admission almost certainly resulted in a more lenient sentence. He received two concurrent sentences for 16 months. He was not required to seek treatment.

Lisa's mother could not deal with what had happened to her daughter. Lisa lived separately from her family of origin, in residential care, for many years after her disclosure. She now lives independently. After a long period of no contact, she sees her mother and siblings regularly. I always admired Lisa's resourcefulness and her commitment to her treatment work. I hope she has continued working and studying towards a professionally rewarding career. I hope she makes peace with her mother. Lisa's mother's strongly-held religious beliefs prevented her from supporting her daughter through the worst time of her life. Lisa's generous spirit, as evidenced by her sharing of her experience in this book, will continue to benefit others.

Jasmine's father denied sexually abusing his daughter, despite her clear verbal accounts and medical evidence indicating that she had been interfered with. Jasmine's mother sought a divorce, and in the matrimonial proceedings, a finding of sexual abuse was made on balance of probability. Jasmine lived with her mother and sister throughout the investigation and civil court proceedings. Jasmine's father had a range of alternative explanations for the evidence, including: a plot by his in-laws to get rid of him; someone else had sexually abused his daughter and she had mistakenly named him; any hypothetical inappropriate touching by him of his daughter's genitals was only accidental.

There was no criminal prosecution despite strong medical evidence of sexual abuse. Jasmine was too young to give evidence in criminal proceedings and did not make a clear verbal disclosure in the formal investigation interview. Jasmine was considered safe in her mother's care. Additional help was offered to facilitate the recovery process. In matrimonial civil proceedings, Jasmine's father's request for contact was denied until Jasmine was old enough to protect herself from him. Kiera, Jasmine's mother, moved on in her life with purpose, resolve and open heart. I know she found someone to walk life's journey with her and provide a good role model for Jasmine and her other daughters.

Asha's stepfather was convicted and sentenced to seven years' imprisonment for sexually abusing Asha. Her mother and extended family all believed her. She remained living at home with her mother and siblings. There were no civil proceedings because Asha's mother protected her and sought a divorce. Asha's mother taught me to be more respectful of children's non-abusing parents and not to rush too quickly to work directly with the child, bypassing a non-abusing parent who really wants to help make things better. Her feedback encouraged me to work more directly with children's non-abusing parents and allow them to play a significant role in their child's recovery. I was impressed by Asha's family's ability to manage the situation and to draw strength from their religious beliefs, and by Asha's focus on her education.

Evelyn, despite disclosing very clearly at age two-and-a-half that her daddy 'fucked her bum', remained living at home with him and her mother. Her parents explained away her disclosure by saying she was hyperactive, she said "fuck" when she meant "smack", and that her constant urinary tract infections were normal. They had professional witnesses who supported them and no further legal action was taken by the local authority. Officially, Evelyn was not sexually abused. There was no criminal prosecution because Evelyn did not repeat in the formal investigation what she had said to the nursery worker. Even if she had done, she would have been too young to participate in a criminal prosecution if the alleged perpetrator had denied committing the offence, which he did. The local authority failed to secure protective measures through civil proceedings. I see many cases like this in my service, where children continue to show signs of being sexually abused until eventually they are believed.

In the first edition of this book, in a discussion of criminal injuries compensation, I described a young woman, Anne, who came into care at 15 following allegations of sexual abuse. She applied to the then Criminal Injuries Compensation Board (CICB) but received a letter saying that they did not consider her to be a victim of a crime of violence. At the time, this was devastating for Anne. She decided not to appeal, as she did not have the emotional energy to carry on fighting to be recognised as a victim of a crime of violence.

Ann remained in the care system. She was not believed by anyone in her family of origin, although the local authority thought, on balance of probability, that she had been sexually abused by her stepfather. She now lives with her two children and battles with depression, which gets on top of her from time to time. She has no contact with her family of origin, who have excluded and ostracised her for disclosing. There was no criminal prosecution because the police did not believe Ann. Her mother agreed for her to be accommodated and then initiated no further contact with her daughter. Ann paid a very high price for disclosing sexual abuse. She was cut off from her family of origin. I have included her in this Afterword because after 15 years of no contact, her youngest brother contacted her. Her stepfather, now widowed, confessed to abusing her, confirming to her brothers and sisters that what she had said all those years ago was true. Ann's capacity for forgiveness is remarkable. She has given up all psychotropic medication after years of battling with serious depression, and is a full-time mother. This example demonstrates that you sometimes need to take a long-term view.

Bonnie's father did not pursue his request for continued access to his daughter. No legal ruling was made in relation to Bonnie's allegation against him. Bonnie's mother and stepfather, and the mother's side of the extended family, all believed Bonnie. There was no criminal prosecution because Bonnie was considered too young to give evidence. There were no civil proceedings regarding child protection because the local authority felt Bonnie was protected by her family. I admired Bonnie's clear instructions for telling off her father and her spirited removal of the bean bag representing him in therapy.

Heston and Norleen remained living with their mother, who was ordered by the court to allow their father to continue to see the children despite her concern that he had sexually abused both of them. The court ruled that there was no evidence, on balance of probability, that sexual abuse had occurred, and thought that the allegation arose out of an acrimonious divorce dispute. Heston and Norleen's mother faced imprisonment if she did not comply with the court order to allow her ex-partner access to their children. I have no idea how she dealt with this threat, but there have been examples of women defying court orders.

Keith was in residential care when he disclosed sexual abuse by a male residential worker. There was no criminal prosecution because of the time lapse between when the abuse occurred and Keith's disclosure. However, there was an internal inquiry which, on balance of probability, believed what Keith had disclosed, and the worker was dismissed. Recognition of abuse in residential settings has received much more attention recently and has been and continues to be the subject of multiple inquiries. This, in turn, has led to changes in recruitment and a more vigilant approach to staff supervision and training. Unfortunately, new episodes of institutional abuse continue to surface. Perhaps this reminds us that complacency is not a very good protective strategy.

Vanessa lived with her mother, who initially believed that her male partner was sexually abusing her baby. There was no criminal prosecution, nor was there any involvement with statutory child protection agencies. The matter was heard in matrimonial proceedings because Vanessa's mother did not want her partner to have any contact with the child. There was no finding of sexual abuse made during the proceedings and contact was granted to the mother's partner. Shortly afterwards, the mother became reconciled with her partner. It can be difficult to maintain belief when it appears there is no evidence. However, it is still important to talk about keeping safe and discuss any concerns as they arise.

Karen disclosed that her stepfather had been sexually abusing her after she had run away from home and was living in a residential unit. Her mother did not believe her. There was no criminal prosecution. Despite Karen's concerns for her younger brothers and sisters, who remained living at home with her mother and the stepfather who had sexually abused her, the local authority did not remove them. Karen was told by her mother that she could not speak to her siblings about her experience of sexual abuse and if she did, she would not be able to see them any more. Karen kept in contact with her siblings, who eventually came to her for help because the same thing was happening to them. Karen was able to protect them, as she was living independently.

Siblings play a significant role in children's lives, but sometimes sexually abused children must think about themselves and their own safety first, and take a longer-term view in relation to their siblings. Kinship care is increasingly being used, and it is just as important to talk about sexual abuse in the extended birth family as it is in foster families.

Kay was removed from her family of origin and placed with foster carers. All her siblings were also removed and placed in separate foster placements. She disclosed experiences of sexual abuse from a number of adults, both male and female, in her extended family, including her father. There was no criminal prosecution. In civil proceedings, no finding was made regarding the allegations of sexual abuse because the general level of care in the family home was so poor that Kay and her siblings could be removed on the grounds of neglect. Kay has no contact with her father or other members of the extended family. She has limited and supervised contact with her siblings and her mother.

This scenario, where other grounds for removal protect the child from further sexual abuse, is very common. This was the case for Kay. Sometimes it means people are reluctant to talk about sexual abuse at all. However, the distorting and disturbing consequences are more likely to continue if there is no discussion to help make sense of and understand what happened.

Many of the above results of disclosures of sexual abuse are very poor in terms of criminal convictions. However, in a significant number of cases, there was a protecting adult who believed the child and was able to help the child begin the recovery process. Where there was a failure to protect, one can only hope the child found the resources to recover and the courage to tell again should the abuse continue. Sexual abuse is unlikely to stop spontaneously, so for Evelyn and Vanessa, who needed protecting adults to intervene on their behalf, it is likely that the sexual abuse would have continued.

There have been campaigns for legal reform. The introduction of video-recorded evidence in criminal proceedings is one result of successful campaigning for changes in the law on sexual offences against children. But it can seem that for every step forward, there remain other impediments. The legal protection offered by criminal proceedings is not uniformly distributed to the whole of the community. The most vulnerable sections of the community – the very young, the physically and intellectually disabled, those who do not have language or who do not have English as a first language, those who have a psychiatric history – are *less* likely to have their cases put forward into the criminal arena and, conversely, *more* likely to be convicted if they are the *subject* of an allegation. In part, the cases are less likely to be put forward in these situations because these children are less likely, or indeed not able, to make clear unequivocal verbal disclosures of sexual abuse.

> I could tell – get things sorted and I can share my
> problems . . . but David can't – like it's all locked up in
> him and he can't let it out. I think that's why he gets
> hyper and hysterical sometimes. I feel sorry for him –
> because I could tell . . . but he still can't tell anyone.
> *Natasha*

The factors listed above are thought to affect the credibility of the witness. Anything that can be construed as making an individual less credible, for whatever justified or unjustified reason, makes it more difficult for a criminal prosecution to be mounted. The False Memory Syndrome backlash has had a serious effect on whether allegations will be taken forward, especially retrospective ones. Additionally, the credibility of expert witnesses has also been harmed by high-profile cases where the integrity of the evidence given has been compromised.[1] Conviction rates for many sexual offences are

---

1   See, for example, an article printed in *The Voice* by Trudi Simpson in April 2008, at
     http://www.voice-online.co.uk/content.php?show=13370.

actually going down despite changes in the law and the way evidence is gathered.

Vulnerable members of the community are more likely to be convicted when they are the subject of an allegation. This is related to the difficulty they may have in mounting a defence against the allegation and also other people's misperceptions about who sexually offends.

In the examples given above, there is a clear indication that the ethnicity and class of the perpetrator have an impact on the punishment the perpetrator receives: Natasha's perpetrator was white – her mother disbelieved Natasha and she was sent away; Lisa's perpetrator was white – he received strong support from professionals and the media, as well as a lenient sentence. His position within the community was never jeopardised. On his return from prison, he continued to attend church. Lisa, on the other hand, became disconnected from her family and no longer attends the church to which they both belonged.

Ann's perpetrator was white – she was not believed by the police or her family and was excluded and ostracised for speaking out; Bonnie's perpetrator was white – there were no civil or criminal proceedings; Karen's perpetrator was white – there was no criminal prosecution and no support from the family – Karen had to remove and support herself; Kay's perpetrator was white – there were no criminal proceedings and no findings of sexual abuse made at civil proceedings; Heston and Norleen's perpetrator was white, they and their mother black African. A court order ruled that their mother faced imprisonment if she denied the perpetrator access to her children. One Black minority ethnic British perpetrator was sent to prison for seven years and the only perpetrator denied access by the courts to his daughter was not white or English, but Mediterranean.

It is important, therefore, that we understand that the way we currently deal with child sexual abuse reflects all the prejudices and inequalities that exist in our society. Child sexual abuse does not happen in a vacuum. It comes out of the society in which we live. If we are to reduce the risk of sexual abuse and more successfully overcome its effects, we must also tackle the broader inequalities that exist. We need to challenge the abuse of authority that underpins exploitation of vulnerable groups in our society. Potential protectors need to widen the issue of child protection to include not only sexual abuse but all other forms of abuse, including the emotional and sometimes physical violence that accompanies racial and sexual harassment.

An experience of sexual abuse is an extension of the pervasive sexually aggressive culture in which we live. The experience can either confirm for the child that the world is, indeed, made up of the abused and the abusing, or it can challenge the child to find the alternatives.

We should encourage children to participate in protecting each other as well as themselves, to foster a sense of joining together to avoid being solely dependent on the powerful adult who can protect, but who can also abuse.

> **Paula, my friend, came to protect me . . . she would press the horn if he tried anything.**
> *Lisa*

As protectors, we also need to help children learn not to bully and abuse others, particularly when children have been taught to target vulnerable members of the community in order to attack and exploit them. We need to try and stop other adults teaching children to adopt such inequalities and prejudices. Children learn about institutionalised hatred from the adults around them, and adults should take responsibility for monitoring and challenging other adults when we see such views being fostered.

Child sexual abuse is complex, and ways of bringing it to light and dealing with it are often complicated and unpredictable. Very clear information about sexual abuse, how to recognise it, how to reduce the risk of it happening to children, and how to minimise its effects, should be given to children, parents and every adult who comes into contact with children in their day-to-day lives.

We need sensitive monitoring that can identify children who may be more vulnerable to sexual abuse because of previous experiences of sexual abuse, their position within the wider community or the behaviour of their parents. We need services that will help children who have been sexually abused to tell and get the help they need to recover. Protecting adults have an essential role to play in dealing with sexual abuse. Professional child protection agencies will only ever deal with a minority of cases – usually those where the situation is extremely serious and community interventions have failed to help.

It is vital that the wider community is actively involved in the task of protecting children. For children from the dominant ethnic group there will be a greater number of positive images for them to aspire to, whereas children from minority ethnic groups have to cope with unhelpful racist stereotyping. An experience of sexual abuse can make a child want to reject fundamental aspects of their identity, which can include gender and ethnicity. It can also, as we have seen, jeopardise the child's place in the wider community. Strong protective adults from the child's own community are important role models for the child. They are key to ensuring a positive and successful resolution of an experience of sexual abuse that does not jeopardise the child's future within their community.

Sexually abusive behaviour is unacceptable and we all need to do everything we can to make sure it is not allowed to flourish. Only organised networks of protecting adults will effectively outmanoeuvre sex offenders. Haphazard, individualistic responses are unlikely to stop or reduce the risk of sexual abuse in the long term for the majority of children.

This book has sought to: inform children and protecting adults about the risks of sexual abuse; teach the responsible exercise of authority; describe how to express anger and outrage safely and constructively; and develop safer communities for children and their protectors. It moves on to discuss the healing process and the consequences of trauma so we can truly understand the lifelong trajectory of our childhood experiences, both good and bad.

Getting support for yourself and your child may often be the first step towards establishing a network and experiencing a sense of community. Being in contact with children puts adults in touch with a child's perspective and also with other adults who care for children. Those adults, in turn, may be more receptive to concerns regarding the safety of children than you think. Fostering should be part of wider community activity and support.

Tragedies involving children, such as the death of Jamie Bulger, abducted while shopping with his mother and then murdered by his juvenile abductors, serve to highlight the need for confident intervention in challenging inappropriate behaviour in public. Jamie Bulger would have been 18 this year, had we been more vigilant and able to prevent his abduction. This year, his mother, Denise Fergus, launched an appeal for a Red Balloon Learning Centre for children bullied in school, to be set up in Merseyside.[2] Working towards a safer future for any one child should mean a safer future for all children. The monitoring and supervision you provide for your child or for children you come into contact with should extend to other children and, in turn, influence the other adults with whom they come into contact. Sharing the responsibility to protect ultimately strengthens the protective network.

Understanding the reality of the experience of sexual abuse will help you to discover your own capacity to protect. Through protecting others, you come to know your own authority; find the strength to bear witness; the courage to speak out; the compassion that fosters healing, openness and a loving heart; and the inspiration to allow

2   see www.redballoonlearner.com.

children and young people to move to forgiveness and to keep:

> *these hands you once ill treated*
> *with all their tenderness intact.*[3]

3   From *Revenge*, by Luis Enrique Mejia Godoy, translated by Dinah Livingston, a song
     based on lyrics to Tomas Borge, addressed to his jailors and torturers. Published in *Poems
     for Refugees* (2002), London: Vintage.

Appendix

This appendix lists several useful organisations and resources, but much more information can be found on the internet. Internet safety is important and all sites listed here provide help to keep safe.

Useful organisations

The following organisations provide an array of resources for families where sexual abuse is an issue, or they have specialist knowledge about an aspect that has been raised in the book. The organisations can signpost you to specific resources that may be helpful.

We only list head offices, but your telephone directory may list a local branch.

Association for Family Therapy

www.aft.org.uk

AFT is the leading body representing those working with families in the public and independent sector in the UK. The broad group of therapies under the banner of "systemic family therapy" work not only with families, but with individual children and adults, couples, and the wider communities of clients. They work in ways that not only support change with individuals but also in their relationships in the family and beyond, so children, young people and/or those important to them are supported in continued recovery.

BAAF
Saffron House
6–10 Kirby Street
London EC1N 8TS
Tel: 020 7421 2600
www.baaf.org.uk
Provides support to those who have been adopted and separated from their birth family. It also gives advice to foster and adoptive parents and has a number of publications including books, DVDs/videos and training courses or parenting sexually abused children, trauma and recovery, and safe caring.

Barnardo's
Tanners Lane
Barkingside, Ilford
Essex IG6 1QG
Tel: 020 8550 8822
www.barnardos.org.uk
Produces books, leaflets and other resources available for carers to use for advice and help caring for children, as well as publications and games for children. It runs a number of projects in conjunction with the community. It runs programmes for foster families and for children who are vulnerable. Provides counselling for children.

Child Abuse Studies Unit
University of North London
62–66 Ladbroke House
Highbury Grove
London N5 2AD
Tel: 020 7133 5014
www.cwasu.org
Offers information, advice and training on all aspects of child abuse.

Children's Legal Centre
University of Essex
Wivenhoe Park
Colchester CO4 3SQ
Advice line: 0845 345 4345
Publications, Sales and
Administration: 01206 872 466
www.childrenslegalcentre.com
A unique, independent national charity concerned with law and
policy affecting children and young people. The Centre has many
years of experience in providing legal advice and representation to
children, their carers and professionals throughout the UK.

ChildLine
Weston House
42 Curtain Road
London EC2A 3NH
Tel: 0800 1111
NSPCC Asian Child Protection Helpline: 0800 096 7719
www.childline.org.uk
The website is aimed mostly at children and teenagers. Some
questions about sexual abuse and why it happens are answered. The
topics of emotional, physical and sexual abuse are covered. A video
about the importance of talking about problems, hosted by
YouTube, is available. ChildLine number is provided for children to
talk about their problems with a councillor. The site is also available
in Welsh.

Criminal Injuries Compensation Authority
Tay House
300 Bath Street
Glasgow G2 4LN
Tel: 0800 358 3601
www.cica.gov.uk

Family Rights Group
18 Ashwin Street
London E8 3DL
Tel: 020 7923 2628
Advice line: 0800 731 1696
www.frg.org.uk

Kidscape
2 Grosvenor Gardens
London SW1W 0DH
Tel: 020 7730 3300
Helpline: 08451 205 204
www.kidscape.org.uk
Offers training programmes for use in schools to help children
learn about keeping safe by role playing difficult situations and
developing coping strategies and the confidence to tell a trusted
adult.

MOSAC
141 Greenwich High Road
London SE10 8JA
Helpline: 0800 980 1958
www.mosac.org.uk
Telephone helpline for parents and carers. Factsheets available on
the issue of sexual abuse and self-harm; many provide help with
court cases. Telephone numbers provided for a large number of
support organisations on a wide range of issues. Can recommend
several books about the issue. The website is aimed at carers and
parents.

National Society for the Prevention of Child Cruelty (NSPCC)
Weston House
42 Curtain Road
London EC2A 3NH
ChildLine: 0800 1111
NSPCC Asian Child Protection Helpline: 0800 096 7719

Telephone support for adults/carers of sexually abused children:
0808 800 5000
www.nspcc.org.uk
Website sections available for parents and for under-18s. Also
available in Welsh and other languages – click on the other
languages at the bottom of the home page.

Rape Crisis Centre

www.rapecrisis.org.uk
Many centres run survivors groups and support and advice to
mothers of children who have been sexually abused. Check your
local telephone directory.

There-4-Me

www.there4me.com
Associated with the NSPCC, aimed at 12–16-year-olds and designed
to be a site where children can find information about a number of
issues, including sexual health. Counsellors are available to talk to
children online. Message boards available for children to talk about
a number of issues. Very large and wide range of additional contacts
and sites provided, all aimed at children and teens, covering a wide
range of issues such as teen alcoholism, anger management and
depression.

Voice

Rooms 100–106
Kelvin House
RTC Business Centre
London Road
Derby DE24 8UP
Tel: 01332 291 042
Helpline: 0845 122 8695
www.voiceuk.org.uk
A national self-help action group for young people with learning
disabilities and their families coping with the issues surrounding
sexual abuse. Campaigns for legal reforms.

Voices from Care

39 The Parade
Roath
Cardiff CF24 3AD
Tel: 029 2045 1431
www.voicesfromcarecymru.org.uk
Formerly the National Association of Young People in Care.

The Who Cares? Trust

Kemp House
152–160 City Road
London EC1V 2NP
Tel: 020 7251 3117
www.thewhocarestrust.org.uk
Produces two publications for looked after children and young
people – *Who Cares?* (for those aged 10 to 18) and *KLiC!* (for those
aged 8 to 12). See website for details.

Women's Support Project

www.womenssupportproject.co.uk
This is a confidential voluntary organisation that offers support,
information and training on all aspects of abuse. They also have a
resource library. Services for deaf women and their children have
been developed.

Young Minds

48–50 St John Street
London EC1M 4DG
Tel: 020 7336 8445
www.youngminds.org.uk
Site is split into sections for children, teenagers and parents. Advice
is given on a range of issues. Adult's section focuses on support for
carers and offers advice for caring for young people. Telephone
helplines are provided for each group.

Groups for survivors of sexual abuse

Barnardo's Mosaic Project
75 Osborne Road
Jesmond
Newcastle-upon-Tyne NE2 2AN
Tel: 0191 212 0237
www.barnardos.org.uk
Barnardo's Mosaic project works with children who have been
sexually abused, with the aim of building up the child's self-esteem
and resilience to help them fulfil their potential.

Basement Project
PO Box 5
Abergavenny NP7 5XW
Tel: 01873 856524
www.basementproject.co.uk
The Basement Project provides support groups for those who have
been abused as children and people who self-harm.
Aimed at teens and adults who self-harm and have suffered abuse.
Produces factsheets and publications about self-harm and on
surviving abuse. Website is available in Welsh and English.

Incest Survivors Aberdeen
Is a Scottish Charity dedicated to adult survivors of childhood sexual
abuse both male and female, and their supporters. Hosted by
Beehive to give you some protection while searching for helpful
resources and information.
http://beehive.thisisnorthscotland.co.uk/default.asp?WCI=SiteHome&
ID=2892

ISAS – Incest and Sexual Abuse Survivors
Is a Nottinghamshire based registered charity that provides face to
face, telephone and group counselling services for adult male and
female survivors of childhood sexual abuse, their partners and family
members
http://www.isas-notts.org.uk/

NAPAC

Is the National Association for People Abused in Childhood. It is a registered charity, based in the UK, providing support and information for people abused in childhood
http://www.napac.org.uk/

S:VOX

Is a new national organisation, created to address issues that affect survivors of any form of violence and abuse, be that physical, emotional, sexual or spiritual, experienced in childhood or adulthood. They run self-help weekends at least annually and an email forum for survivors who have attended the self-help groups at Greenbelt. http://www.greenbelt.org.uk
http://www.svox.org.uk/

The Survivors Trust

Is a national umbrella agency for over 125 specialist voluntary sector agencies providing a range of counselling, therapeutic and support services working with women, men and children who are victims/survivors of rape, sexual violence and childhood sexual abuse.
http://www.thesurvivorstrust.org

Books

Many relevant books and leaflets can be found on the websites noted above.

Directory and Book Services

www.dabsbooks.co.uk
A specialist book and information service for people who are overcoming childhood abuse, sexual abuse, or domestic violence, and for those who live or work with them.

Videos

Many relevant videos can be found on the websites listed below.

www.mediarights.com

www.viewtech.co.uk

Both of these sites provide a very wide range of videos for both
carers and for children. Type in your search term to find lists of
relevant titles.